How to Write an Essay
A Guide for Business Management Students
Alnoor F. Alnoor
MBA, BA, F.Inst.A.M (Adv.Dip), C.Dip.A.F

How to Write an Essay

Copyright © 2018 by Alnoor F Alnoor

First edition July 2018

All rights reserved. No part of this book may be reproduced, stored in a retrieval system, or transmitted in any form by any means, electronic, mechanical, photocopying, recording or otherwise, except as may be explicitly permitted by the applicable copyright laws or by prior written permission from the author.

Made in the United States of America
ISBN-13: 978-1986146371
ISBN-10: 1986146375

Preface

Business management students face challenges related to generating relevant content for college papers and open-ended, essay-type exams during their years of college study.

This book focuses on fostering their ability to recall knowledge and appropriate vocabulary in a systematic manner that helps in establishing the skeleton of the content and determining main points, headings, and sub-headings. This ultimately fosters the flow of writing and leads to better coverage of the topic. The book further contains a practical lexicon that provides a carefully-selected list of essential business management terms in addition to condensed, direct-to-the-point chapters on relevant topics such as the communication process, effective business writing, the management model, key words and action verbs, and the examination technique.

Therefore, in addition to providing an effective writing tool, the book is also a condensed multi-disciplinary reference book that hones various skills and knowledge bases. It creates for students a solid foundation that they may carry into their professional life.

I hope that the book would be useful for undergraduate business management students throughout the world. It is particularly useful for those in countries where English is the medium of education but is not the mother tongue. In this respect, it helps their transition into the study of the courses in English.

The ideas presented here have culminated from many years of theoretical studies, practical experience, and creative thinking. I hope that they will contribute to the business and management library and form a creative and useful approach to address the challenges of writing. I also hope that these ideas will be enhanced by further discussion and publication in this area.

Alnoor F. Alnoor

Contents

Preface..5

Introduction..8

Part One

The Backgroun..11

Introduction..13

Chapter 1

The Challenges of Open-Ended, Essay-Type Exam Questions.................14

Chapter 2

 Background Research..16

Part Two

The Components of the Technique 19

Introduction..21

Chapter 3

The Concept of Association..22

Chapter 4

The 6 Ws & O (The Ambit)...25

Chapter 5

The Management Model, Key Words, and Action Verbs..........33

Chapter 6

The Communication Process 44

Chapter 7

Business Writing 49

Chapter 8

The Examination Technique 52

Part Three

Utilizing the Ambit Technique 55

Introduction 57

Chapter 9

The Ambit Technique Recap 58

Chapter 10

The Process: Utilizing the Ambit Technique At the Exam 60

Part Four

The Practical Lexicon for Business Management 65

Introduction 67

Chapter 11

The Lexicon 69

Appendixes 104

Appendix 1

McNally High Frequency Words 105

Appendix 2

Statistics about Word Usage in the Book 106

Appendix 3

Past Examination Questions 109

Question 2 112

Question 3 114

Question 7 123

Appendix 4

Writing Template Using the Aspects and Depths....................................127

Acknowledgments...133

About the Author...134

Introduction

"The true lover of knowledge is always striving after being."
-Plato-

As a management student, I used to wonder that even though I had thoroughly studied and revised, the "open" essay questions always posed a challenge. How can I determine all the pertinent points, issues, or arguments to ensure complete, or at least, substantial coverage?

Our minds often need a trigger to recall relevant facts and information in a systematic manner. We need a mechanism to stimulate the questioning processes, recalling of information, and linking of ideas. We further need a clear vocabulary with which to express our ideas.

The business management and communication domains are rich with many established techniques and concepts as well as impressive books, some of which have inspired this work. However, many of these concepts and techniques focus on a particular subject or topic, and none may alone provide a more comprehensive tool that helps with generating the content. Examples of these are:

– The Examination Technique: a time management tool
– Effective writing skills: focuses on style, grammar, and overall approach
– Communication process: deals with the elements of communication, e.g. message, sender, and receiver, as well as communication barriers

Therefore, what I needed, and what many students needed, was something more. We needed a tool that helps us to generate the content itself. To that end, the Ambit Technique provided in this book utilizes the concept of association, the 6 Ws, the Management Model and key words, together with essential vocabulary to help with generating the content in a systematic manner.

This technique is based on associating key words to related concepts or ideas. Association is an established concept in the field of psychology and is used in memory-improving techniques.

The design of this book entailed focusing on practical issues and rules of thumb wherever possible. To foster readability, discussion of the topics has been brief and direct. I have resorted to elaboration only when required, and to the extent necessary to explain the relevance and roles of the components within the technique.

The book is divided into four parts.

Part 1 discusses the background of the technique, and consists of two chapters. Chapter 1 discusses the challenges of essay-type, open-ended exam questions and sheds some light on how a systematic approach can help mitigate them. Chapter 2 briefly discusses a background research on the use of English language words and explains how the Practical Lexicon provided in this book should cover a wide spectrum of business and management topics.

Part 2 is divided into six chapters. Each chapter briefly explains one of the six components of the technique. These components are the Concept of Association; the 6 Ws & O; the Management Model, Key Words, and Action Verbs ; the Communication Process; Business Writing; and the Examination Technique.

Part 3 guides you systematically in two brief chapters toward using the technique.

Part 4 includes the Practical Lexicon for the field of business management and tips on how to use it. This part is also a unique feature of the book, as it provides a concise and useful management dictionary.

Appendix 3 contains past examinations questions from the Institute of Administrative Management - UK (with permission) to provide practical exercises on using the technique. A writing template is provided in appendix 4 for the same purpose,

I hope that the book will be useful for management students, at both the graduate and undergraduate levels, and that it will help them generate appropriate content for essay-type, open-ended management questions, as well as college papers.

Part One
The Background

Introduction

This part is divided into two chapters that briefly discuss the background of the book's idea.

Chapter 1 discusses the challenges involved in essay-type, open-ended exam questions. It sheds some light on what students need and how a systematic approach can meet their needs.

Chapter 2 deals with the background research, which is based on McNally High Frequency Words. It shows how a given number of common words, in addition to essential management vocabulary, can substantially cover a wide spectrum of business management topics and issues.

Chapter 1
The Challenges of Open-Ended, Essay-Type Exam Questions

Writing, in general, is a complex communication process that involves different skills and abilities, and poses different challenges. Answering open-ended questions, in particular, requires a systematic approach to ensure producing an appropriate and comprehensive answer. The aim of this book is to provide business students with the essential vocabulary and a technique that addresses these challenges in a systematic manner.

The challenges encountered by students at the exam are summarized as follows:

1. Tackling an exam paper in an organized and concise manner within a given time (**organization**)[1]. To that end, the content has to be organized according to a plan. The ideas and arguments must flow logically and be presented systematically, one after the other.
2. Recalling and determining the main points, ideas, or arguments to be addressed or covered (**main points**). This is the essential first step of the writing process. Here, the skeleton of the content is drawn, and the logical order of ideas is determined.
3. Associating the main points generated in (2) with other points to trigger more ideas or arguments (**recalling facts**). Each point, idea, or argument should lead to other relevant ones, thus creating the overall framework (or the Ambit) of the content.

---

[1] The words in bold denote the abbreviations used in Table 9.1 in Chapter 9.

4. Adopting an appropriate style and correct grammar, spelling, punctuation, etc. (**style**). This is essential for the readability of any written material. Incorrect grammar or misspelled words may distort the intended meaning altogether.
5. Elaborating on each point, idea, or argument in an orderly manner, using appropriate vocabulary to support the arguments (**vocabulary**). Once students have drawn the overall framework (or the Ambit), they need to explain each point in a reasonably detailed manner. This requires sufficient vocabulary.

Students often resort to extremes in a variety of ways at the exams. On the one hand, they may sometimes fill the answer sheets with too many ideas and arguments in their quest to present a comprehensive answer. This hinders their ability to adopt an organized approach and focus on the main or required points or arguments. The other extreme is manifested by the students' inability to address all the pertinent points, issues, or arguments; thus, they present incomplete answers and subsequently lose marks. These two extremes are depicted to describe the two sides of the problem. In reality, our performance often encompasses a combination of both problems.

Chapter 2
Background Research

In the previous chapter, the challenges of essay-type, open-ended exams were identified, briefly explained, and summarized as follows:

1. Organization
2. Determining main points
3. Recalling facts
4. Style
5. Vocabulary

Points (1) through (4) are mainly concerned with the framework of the content and the appropriate style. Point 5, vocabulary, is the tool with which points, ideas, or arguments are expressed. Without adequate vocabulary, one may not be able to do so, and may waste considerable time striving for the right words.

This chapter discusses the issue of vocabulary and illustrates how the Practical Lexicon provided in this book should substantially cover a wide spectrum of business topics.

Any discipline in the arts or science has a special lingo or vocabulary, the knowledge of which is necessary for mastering the subject or writing about it. In the business field, there are many impressive dictionaries, each aiming at listing almost every word or term that could be encountered. A typical dictionary lists an average of 2000-2500 terms, all of which are indeed useful. However, many are not commonly used or required in the context of every examination or the ordinary content of written material at the workplace. They are rarely used and are needed only when narrow specializations or very specific topics are involved. In addition, many other phrases or terms are obvious, such as bank, bank account, etc.

No one can easily memorize a complete business dictionary. There is a need for a concise, direct, and easily comprehensible list of essential business terms to serve the purpose: a Practical Lexicon. Such a list is provided in this book.

It is amazing how certain common words occur repeatedly in reading material to the extent that they make up a great proportion of various texts. At the two sides of the Atlantic, researchers have proved this phenomenon. The following depicts an example from each side of the ocean.

In the UK, Mr. J. McNally, a former Senior Educational Psychologist from Manchester, and Mr. W. Murray, Headmaster of the former Thirlestaine Court School in Cheltenham, UK, conducted an interesting research, the outcome of which is now used for educational purposes. The following is an excerpt of their findings:

1. Twelve words make up, on average, one-quarter of all readings; these are "a, and, he, I, in, is, it, of, that, the, to, was."
2. Twenty words, together with the above twelve words (thirty-two words total), make up, on average, one-third of all readings; these are "all, as, at, be, but, are, for, had, have, him, his, not, on, one, said, so, they, we, with, you."
3. Sixty-eight words, together with the above thirty-two words (a total of one hundred words), make up, on average, one-half of all readings; examples of these are "about, an, back, which, who, will, your."
4. One hundred and fifty most-used words and nouns, including: "after, again …school …white … would, year."
5. These 250 words make up approximately 70 percent of juvenile readings and about 60 percent of adult readings.

The list is currently known as *McNally High Frequency Words*. The complete list of words (now published as 247 words) is depicted in Appendix (1).

In the U.S., a similarly interesting list of the top 250 words was produced by the website www.anglik.com, an online resource for students of English as a second language. In this list, the words are listed in order of rank, starting with the word "the" as the most used word, followed by the words "of, to, and, a, in, is, it," and ending with the words "night, real, life, few, and stop" at the bottom of the list.

This list has noticeable similarities to the McNally list, and substantiates the basic assertion that a great proportion of various texts is made up of a limited number of repetitive words.

Similarly, in the business domain, the basic and essential vocabulary occurs frequently within business-related texts to the extent that it makes up a significant proportion of them.

This leads to a logical inference. If 250 common words make up, on average, 60 percent of adult readings, then the Practical Lexicon for the business management provided in this book, which consists of 307 words, should substantially cover, together with other common English words, a wide spectrum of business topics and issues.

To illustrate this, Appendix 2 gives statistics about word usage in this work. It shows how a certain number of management terms, together with other common English words, have made up a substantial proportion of the book's text.

This leads to the assertion that, in most cases, if not all, a carefully selected set of vocabulary, together with the Ambit Technique provided in this book, should provide you with robust tools that will help you create a better content in different respects.

Part Two

The Components of the Technique

Introduction

The Ambit Technique is comprised of six components. This part briefly explains each in a separate chapter:

Chapter 3: The Concept of Association

Chapter 4: The 6 Ws & O (The Ambit)

Chapter 5: The Management Model, Key Words, and Action Verbs

Chapter 6: The Communication Process

Chapter 7: Business Writing

Chapter 8: The Examination Technique

Chapter 3
The Concept of Association

Memory and the mechanisms of the human mind have been the focus of considerable research and scholarly works. Many concepts, theories, and arguments have been developed, and books written, creating a massive and interesting body of knowledge. Association and its role in the mechanism of memory was one of these developments. It refers to "the process of forming mental connections or bonds between sensations, ideas, ormemories."[1]

During my childhood back in Africa, I accompanied my mother one summer day to visit a friend of hers in the neighboring block. When we were welcomed into the house, a large flower tree captured my attention. I was infatuated by the beauty and aroma of its flowers. I stretched my tiny body to reach for the branches, picked a flower, and smelled it deeply.

Almost thirty years later, during my services for an oil company in the Middle East, I was given an assignment in a remote industrial city. Walking around the housing compound one hot summer day, I saw the same tree perking up above the fence of a house. The flowers were stretching over the fence. At that same moment, I remembered my mother, and recalled the shape of that house we visited in the neighboring block back in Africa.

---

1 The use of the following words in this chapter is based on the definitions of Merriam-Webster's Collegiate Dictionary. 1) Association: 3: something linked in memory or imagination with a thing or person. 4: the process of forming mental connections or bonds between sensations, ideas, or memories.; 2) Associate: 4: to bring together or into relationship in any of various intangible ways (as in memory or imagination).; 3) Memory: 1a: the power or process of reproducing or recalling what has been learned and retained esp. through associative mechanisms b: the store of things learned and retained from an organism's activity or experience as evidenced by modification of structure or behavior or by recall and recognition 2b: the fact or condition of being remembered 3a: a particular act of recall or recollection b: an image or impression of one that is remembered.; 4) Memorize: to commit to memory; learn by heart; 5) Remind: to put in mind of something; cause to remember; 6) Remember: 1: to bring to mind or think of again 4: to retain in memory 1: to exercise or have the power of memory 2: to have a recollection or remembrance; 7) Recall: 1b: to bring back to mind c: to remind one of 3: remembrance of what has been learned or experienced

Since then, I have traveled to many places for work, study, tourism, and permanent immigration. I have had numerous experiences and encounters of pain and joy, failure and success. Yet, I still recall the same memory every time I see that flower or smell its fragrance anywhere in the world. What had actually happened was association. The moment I was captivated by that tree and its beautiful flowers, I subconsciously associated it with that house and the joyful company of my mother.

We learn through the five senses, i.e., seeing, hearing, smelling, tasting, and touching. What we learn thereby is stored in our memory. At times we forget, i.e., fail to recall some of what we learned in different ways, through different methods and media. That includes the things we had deliberately studied to prepare for an exam or to learn a profession.

Often, we recall a memory or a piece of information upon exposure to an object that is related or can be associated to it. In other words, an object that reminds us of the original exposure. Surprisingly, we might at times recall a memory or a piece of information upon the exposure to something that is apparently unrelated. The fragrance of a particular perfume, for example, may remind us of a place. What actually happened is that the perfume may have reminded us of a person, who in turn has reminded us of that particular place.

A distinction has to be made between subconscious and conscious association. The former denotes, as the term implies, the associations made subconsciously during our encounters in daily life. The latter one refers to the deliberate association that we make to memorize something.

The Concept of Association has been a cornerstone of most techniques of memory improvement. Such techniques help us to memorize things like long numbers, names, foreign words, etc. by associating them to things we already know or remember.

In their interesting book on the subject, The Memory Book, Lorayne and Lucas (1996) state that "all memory, whether trained or untrained, is based on association;" and "…you should realize that you've used association all your life. The problem is that you've usually associated subconsciously, without realizing the association for what it was. Anything you clearly associated, even subconsciously, is sure to have been easily remembered. But since you have no control over your subconscious, association has been a hit-or-miss kind of thing all your life."

Their technique focuses on memorizing. The Ambit Technique provided in this book is a way to foster systematic recalling of the information that was memorized. Both systems rely on Association. The memorizing techniques, on the one hand, rely on associating a series of pieces of information to one another. Should you need to memorize names of persons or places, for example, you need to associate each name with something you already know or remember. With the Ambit Technique, you need to associate the key words with relevant management concepts of which you should already be aware. As such, Association is a two-way process. First, during our voyage of learning something, we associate what we are studying to something we already know or can easily recall. Second, in our return trip, while trying to recall what we studied, we utilize association through objects, concepts, etc., i.e., what we already know, to link us to the information we need to recall. Hence, the moment you determine the key words that are relevant to the topic in question, association should take place. Under each key word, you should be able to list a number of key points around which you can build your answer, report, etc. This process shall further be fostered by utilizing the 6 Ws & O (explained in the next chapter,) which should help you trigger more questions and queries to achieve better coverage of the pertinent aspects of the topic or issue.

Students need to study and memorize the various management topics as well as the key words. During revision, they should make an association between the key words and the topic being revised. During the exam, the association made should help recall the various concepts related to the individual key words, which should in turn generate more related concepts, such as subheadings, and so on. To facilitate this association, the key words given in this book have been sorted, according to their relationship to key functions and concepts in the Management Model preceding the list. The 6 Ws & O, as stated earlier, play an important role in making the association.

Once you have finished reading all the briefings on the components of the Ambit Technique, Part 3 shall help guide you systematically toward using it.

Finally, this component of the technique, in this context, cannot be treated as a separate mechanism that acts alone. Its role is implicit within the overall framework of the technique, and results from the interactivity of the other components, especially the key words and the 6 Ws & O.

Chapter 4
The 6 Ws & O (The Ambit)

Simply speaking, the 6 Ws are the basic questions in any known language. Being six in number, and having the letter "W" as a denominator, they are widely known as the 6 Ws, though are sometimes called the 5 "Ws" and an H. These are: What, When, Why, Who, Where, and How. In the Ambit Technique, the word "Outcome", abbreviated as "O", has been added to this set of questions. This addition aims to accommodate the evaluation of the expected results, outcomes, or pros and cons, whenever applicable, of a given issue, action, or proposal.

In management, the 6 Ws are commonly used to help identify the different aspects of a topic or situation. In some works on business communications, for instance, they are recommended as a tool that helps in composing a complete message. They are particularly used in Method Study to question the existing arrangements and methods of doing work, to trigger further questions, and to help generate ideas. Examples of such uses are:

- What is being done? What is its purpose (why)? What is the problem? What are its causes (why)? What is the objective? What else can be done or achieved, and why?
- When do activities/tasks take place, and why? When else can such activities take place, and why?
- How are the activities/tasks performed, and why? How else can they be performed, and why?
- Who performs the activities/tasks, and why? Who else can perform them, and why?

- Where do the activities/tasks take place, and why? Where else can the activities/tasks take place, and why?
- Why: As shown above, it denotes the causes of a problem, reasons behind a particular setting or situation, and reasons/justifications for particular alternative solutions or recommendations.
- Outcome or "O": What are the expected or targeted outcomes of this exercise, and how do we evaluate them? What are the advantages and disadvantages of the recommended solutions?

The Concept of the Ambit:

This book argues that almost every issue or topic has an Ambit encompassing certain aspects. These aspects are mainly: definition or identification of the issue or topic; spatial and timing aspects; the people involved; the reasons for its occurrence or prevalence; the way it happens or takes place; and its outcomes or consequences.

The term Ambit originates from and corresponds to the 6 Ws and O. In conjunction with other components of the technique, particularly the Management Model and Key Words, it can trigger more questions, key points, and ideas, as shall be explained in the next chapter.

In the context of this technique, the term Ambit is defined as: *A framework of inquiry that comprises the aspects, which can possibly be involved, or required to be addressed, within an issue or topic, and that aims to help achieving complete coverage of that issue or topic.*

To illustrate the relationship of the Ambit with the 6 Ws & O, Table 4.1 briefly describes each of the aspects of the Ambit and how they correspond to the 6 Ws and O.

Table 4.1

Aspects of the Ambit

ASPECT	6 Ws & O	DESCRIPTION
Definition/ Identification	What is it?	Definition/identification of the problem, issue, object, etc.
Spatial Aspect	Where?	Location, layout, or distance involved.
Timing Aspect	When?	The time framework of the operation or issue in question.
People Involved	Who?	The doers, beneficiaries, or those affected.
Reasons	Why?	The causes of the problem, issue, etc.; the objectives or justifications.
The Way it Happens or Takes Place	How?	Methods, approaches, systems, etc.; and the means of doing it, e.g., machine, material, etc.
Outcomes/ Consequences	O	The benefits, outcomes, costs, or consequences, etc. – current, expected or desired.

Further, in today's management practice, several techniques have been developed to explore the various dimensions, scope, or magnitude of a given situation, problem, or circumstance. A careful analysis of these techniques reveals that the elements they use correspond either explicitly or implicitly to certain aspects of the Ambit. However, these techniques differ from the Ambit in that each one of them is confined to a particular activity, situation, or concept, while the Ambit is a comprehensive concept that can accommodate most situations.

To illustrate how the Ambit could cover, either explicitly or implicitly, the aspects of different issues or topics, let us examine some of these methods or techniques.

1. The Four Os of Purchasing:

This technique is used by firms as a tool to establish their marketing mix. It comprises the pertinent elements of a purchase on the part of the consumer or buyer. The function of the Four Os vis-à-vis the aspects of the Ambit is depicted in Table 4.2.

Table 4.2
The Four Os of Purchasing

ELEMENT	DESCRIPTION
Objects	The product/s
Objectives	The usefulness, functions, or utility of the product
Organization	The people in charge of the purchases
Operations	The procurement systems, procedures, or practices followed by the purchaser

Results obtained by utilizing the Ambit:

AMBIT ASPECT	DESCRIPTION	RELEVANT Os
Definition/ Identification	Definition/identification of the problem, issue, object, etc.	Objects
Spatial Aspect	Location, layout, or distance involved.	Implicit in "Operations"
Timing Aspect	The time framework of the operation or issue in question.	Implicit in "Operations"
People involved	The doers, beneficiaries, or those affected.	Organization
Reasons	Causes of the problem, issue, etc.; the objectives or justifications.	Objectives
The Way it Happens / Takes Place	Methods, approaches, systems, etc; and the means of doing it, e.g., machine, material, etc.	Operations
Outcomes/ Consequences	The benefits, outcomes, or costs – current, expected, or desired.	Objectives

2. The Five Ms:

This is another technique used by firms to ensure that all aspects pertinent to the solution of a problem at the workplace are taken into account. It is comprised of five elements: men, machine, material, measurement, and method. Similarly, a careful analysis of these five elements reveals their correspondence to the aspects of the Ambit. Table 4.3 illustrates the functions of the Five Ms as compared to the aspects of the Ambit.

Table 4.3
The Five Ms

ELEMENT	DESCRIPTION
Men	The people who do the job
Machine	The equipment, machinery, etc., that is used or needed
Material	The material used or needed
Measurement	Quantities of various inputs and outputs
Method	The way work is or should be done

Results obtained by utilizing the Ambit:

AMBIT ASPECT	DESCRIPTION	RELEVANT Ms
Definition/ Identification	Of the problem or issue involved.	N/A1
Spatial Aspect	Location, layout, or distance involved.	Implicit in "Method"
Timing Aspect	The time framework of the operations.	Implicit in "Method"
People involved	The doers, beneficiaries, or those affected.	Workers, customers
Reasons	The causes of the problem, issue, etc.; the objectives or justifications.	N/A2
The ways it happens/takes place	Methods, approaches, systems, etc.; and the means of doing it, e.g., machine, material, etc.	Method Machine Material
Outcomes/ Consequences	The benefits, outcomes, or costs – current, expected, or desired.	Measurement

Notes:

1. It is assumed that the problem or issue has been identified prior to using the Five Ms.
2. Reasons are not explicitly accommodated in the Five Ms, but should be revealed upon investigating each of them.

3. The Four Ps of Marketing:

To further examine the comprehensiveness of the aspects of the Ambit, let us explore this technique. The Four Ps of Marketing encompasses the four elements of the Marketing Mix, i.e., product, price, promotion, and place. The relationship of these four elements to the aspects of the Ambit is shown in Table 4.4.

Table 4.4

The Four Ps of Marketing

ELEMENT	DESCRIPTION
Product	The commodity being sold and its benefits, uses, functions, and characteristics
Price	The different pricing issues/considerations, including cost, profit margins, retail price, discounts, etc.
Promotion	The measures a firm takes to foster its image and promote its products to increase demand. These include advertising, sales promotion, discounts, direct marketing, etc.
Place	The circulation and delivery of the commodity to the ultimate consumers. It entails using distribution channels like wholesalers and retailers.

Results obtained by utilizing the Ambit:

AMBIT ASPECT	DESCRIPTION	RELEVANT Ps
Definition/Identification	Definition/identification of the problem, issue, object, etc.	Product
Spatial Aspect	Location, layout, or distance involved.	Place/promotion
Timing Aspect	The time framework of the operation or issue in question.	Implicit in "Promotion"
People involved	The operatives, supervisors, etc.	Implicit in "Promotion", i.e., consumers
Reasons	The causes of the problem, issue, etc.; the objectives or justifications	Included in "Promotion", i.e., objectives
The ways it happens/ takes place	Methods, approaches, systems, etc.; and the means of doing it, e.g., advertising, discounts, etc.	Promotion Place
Outcomes/Consequences	The benefits, outcomes, or costs – current, expected, or desired.	Price/profit

It worth noting that while the Ambit covers the aspects of almost every issue or topic, not all issues or topics involve all the aspects. Moreover, and as stated earlier, the Ambit Technique is a tool of writing. It is not a substitute for knowledge and proper preparation. Some exam questions are confined to a specific concept, principle, or definition that needs to be learned by heart. Questions on motivation theories, accounting principles, or principles of management are a few examples. Such topics, though, do involve some of the aspects of the Ambit. Motivation theories, for instance, are concerned with people (who) and their behavioral patterns, i.e., the way it happens (how) and (why) people behave the way they do. In addition, each theory needs to be explained or defined, and its pros and cons (consequences) identified. In such cases, however, spatial and timing aspects are not explicitly involved.

The following examination question from the Institute of Administrative Management (UK) is an example of the topics that involve specific knowledge:

"The application of ergonomics in an organization involves much more than just making sure Health and Safety regulations are being followed. Discuss."

First, you need to know the specific meaning of ergonomics. Second, you need to be aware of the various factors and considerations involved in its application. However, the Ambit can give you guidance. Start with defining the term ergonomics. Then explore its spatial and timing aspects and its impact on the people involved. Further, consider the reasons, objectives, and the way of applying ergonomics. Finally, explore its outcomes and benefits, which include better working conditions, fewer injuries, employees' satisfaction, and increased productivity. Later in this book, you shall learn how to use the Ambit in conjunction with key words.

However, if you were required to make your own definition of something, then exploring all the aspects of the Ambit, one after the other, is very helpful. It enables you to recall, in a systematic manner, what you know about that thing or subject. Exploring each aspect of the Ambit shall lead you to recall certain facts about the subject, which you shall write down. Once you have explored all the aspects, you shall have the pertinent facts that you need to make your definition. All that you shall need to do then is to merge these facts in proper sentences to phrase your definition.

Example 4.1 illustrates this process.

Example 4.1
Using the Ambit

Question: Define "Bank."
First, you need to explore the aspects of the Ambit and try to associate each one to what you know about banks. A careful analysis shall culminate in a result similar to the following:
1. Definition/identification: a financial institution 2. Spatial aspect: bank branches are usually sited at convenient locations 3. Timing aspect: services usually provided during business hours 4. People involved: financial professionals helping businesses and individuals 5. Reasons: to help customers organize their financial matters, and to make financial gains. 6. The Way it Happens: by employing sophisticated financial systems 7. Outcome/Consequences: mutual financial benefits for both the bank and its customers
Second, you may now merge these aspects in a logical manner. Consequently, the definition of "Bank" should look close to this: **"A bank is a financial institution that employs financial professionals and applies sophisticated financial systems for the ultimate goal of helping businesses and individuals organize their financial affairs, and making mutual financial gains. It usually provides its services during business hours through branches at convenient locations."**

To summarize, the term Ambit originates from and corresponds to the 6 Ws & O. The concept of the Ambit is comprehensive and is applicable to, and can accommodate, almost every topic or issue. The elements of other management techniques, exemplified above, that are aimed to tackle specific issues or situations, fall under the "umbrella" of the Ambit in one way or another.

Hence, to ensure appropriate coverage of an issue or topic, you need to carefully explore all the aspects of the Ambit (the 6 Ws & O). That shall help you trigger the pertinent questions, obtain the relevant answers, and produce a content that is relevant and within the particular context.

Finally, as can be inferred from Example 4.1, the usefulness of the Ambit is not confined to the field of business alone. It can be utilized in an equally effective manner in numerous other domains and situations.

Chapter 5
The Management Model, Key Words, and Action Verbs

The components of the Ambit Technique are intended to work together to form one tool. The component discussed in this chapter is comprised of the following:
- The Management Model
- The Key Words
- Action Verbs

The Management Model:

The Management Model is a diagram outlining in a condensed form the major issues, roles, and considerations involved in management practice. The benefit of the Model, and what makes it unique, is that it displays in only one diagram the general framework of management practice. It displays, for instance, what is involved at the corporate level. Once the vision and objectives of an organization are determined, a SWOT[1] analysis may be conducted. The SWOT analysis should reveal the strengths, weaknesses, opportunities, and threats to the organization. The findings of such analysis shall form the basis for the corporate planning phase, which entails change management. This in turn involves organizational development, determining the strategic shift, and making decisions on the organization's growth, which involves making decisions on products, markets, prices, consumer orientation, etc. The Model also illustrates the interrelationships between

---
1 Abbreviation for strengths, weaknesses, opportunities, and threats

the different activities and specializations within an organization. It shows, for example, how marketing research, benchmarking, financial controls, etc., constitute feedback for top management to inform the revision of the strategic plans or direction of the organization.

Students with a solid or at least a reasonable background in management will be able to recall many of the details and subtitles under each heading the moment they read the page. It can also be very useful for other readers who want to form a general idea of what is involved in management practice (Figure 5.1).

The List of Key Words":

The List of Key Words is a set of carefully selected words, terms, and phrases that are a denominator in the management field. It is not to be confused with the Practical Lexicon, which refers to the basic and essential vocabulary. Key words are intended to work in conjunction with the Ambit to help elaborate on the headings depicted in the Management Model or those generated by the use of the Ambit. Examples of these key words are alternatives; assumptions; comparisons; constraints; scope; and sources. Each word may generate several ideas and subheadings within the context of the topic or issue.

For the list to be easily comprehendible and contextualized, it has been sorted according to its relationship to the Management Model.

In the previous chapter, a brief account is given on the 6 Ws & O and the Ambit concept that culminates from them. In this chapter, we shall move a step forward and explore the interactivity of the 6 Ws & O with the Key Words. To this end, a simplified exercise is depicted in Example 5.1.

In this simple example, the Key Words can be used as the key points or headings around which an answer may be built. Under each heading, one can generate pertinent questions, issues, and considerations, and can elaborate on these within the context of the question. Then the role of the Outcome or O shall follow. To this end, give an account on the expected advantages, disadvantages, or outcomes of your recommendations in terms of quantity, quality, savings, timing, and give justifications thereof.

Example 5.1
Using the 6 Ws and O with the Key Words

Question: Write a short essay on how you would go about re-engineering a process within an organization.

First step: Identify the best match of Key Words to this topic. Under Process Re-engineering in the Management Model, you shall find the words cost, speed, quality, and productivity. When you use these Key Words with the 6 Ws and O, you can generate numerous questions like the following:

COST:	SPEED:
What are the cost components? Are they the same at all times (When)? Any shift or seasonal variations (When)? Any overtime (When)? Location (Where): A rented facility? Are costs considered high (How much)? Why costs are high? Is it due to inappropriate methods (How)? Or inefficient /untrained staff (Who)? The consequences (O) on prices, sales, etc. What controls are in force? How frequently (When) are they applied? How are they applied: policies and procedures? Who is in-charge of cost control? The pros and cons (O) of these controls.	What is the pace of production? Is it always the same? Any shift or seasonal variations (When)? Is it considered slow? Why is it slow? Is it due to inappropriate methods (How)? Why using this method? Is that due to inefficient or untrained staff (Who)? Does slowness occur during a certain shift (When)? How to mitigate the problem? By shift re-arrangement (When), staff training (Who) or improving methods (How)? What technology is in use? What are its pros and cons in terms of cost, speed, quality of production, and productivity (O)?
QUALITY:	**PRODUCTIVITY:**
What are the standards? How far are they met? How are Quality Assurance and Quality Control implemented? Reasons for low quality, if any (Why)? What impacts low quality has on sales? Who are the people, or processes, involved?	How productive is the process? Any shift or seasonal variations (When)? Reasons (Why) for low productivity? How to improve productivity? Who is involved? How motivated are they? Is the layout (Where) appropriate? What are the product cycles (When)? What methods (How) are used? And Why?

It can be noticed in Example 5.1 that some of the questions or points generated through this exercise are overlapping. Such overlaps need to be excluded as appropriate. It can also be noted that several other key words were generated during the exercise and played a role. Examples of these are *alternatives* and *characteristics*. This shows the logical interrelationship between the Key Words and the issues and questions that the Ambit can generate and leads us to another concept, i.e., The Depths.

The Depths:

As stated earlier, the Ambit is a framework that encompasses the aspects of definition, people involved, and reasons, as well as space, time, how, and outcome/ consequences that are related to an issue or topic. On the other hand, the list of Key Words interacts with the Ambit to generate more ideas. Nine of these words, depicted in Table 5.4, constitute the Depths within the Ambit.

Table 5.4
The Depths

Scope The intentions, objectives, or limits of dealing with an issue or topic, or the degree of coverage or involvement required.	**Factors** The issues, concerns, reasons, or forces that influence or limit the achievement of results, or lead to certain situations or decisions	**Comparisons** The process of contrasting an object against another to establish the differences and similarities between them
Elements The components, parts, or facets of an issue, topic, or object	**Forms/Types** The kinds, categories, or groupings of an object	**Characteristics** The traits, attributes, or quality of an object
Assumptions The postulations, hypotheses, or deductions on which an action is based	**Alternatives** The available options or choices, or the possible courses of action	**Constraints** The prevailing restrictions or limitations, or the controls in force

These Depths enable you to explore the issue or topic in greater depth and view it from different angles. They allow you to make comparisons, think about alternatives, and consider the characteristics. This culminates in a wider and deeper coverage, and thereby takes you extra steps toward substantial coverage of the content. Example 5.2 illustrates this by applying the Depths to the same topic depicted in Example 5.1.

Example 5.2
Applying the Depths

Depths	Relevant issues/questions raised
Scope	Ascertain the scope of the issue or topic. Does it include, for instance, reviewing the technology and machinery in use, or is it confined to improvements within the existing resources and settings?
Assumptions	Establish whether there are certain assumptions involved, or deductions to be made, e.g., abiding by a no-redundancy policy.
Elements	These have been identified as cost, speed, quality, and productivity. Elements within each element need to be identified, e.g., elements of quality include size, weight, performance, etc.
Factors	Explore the factors involved, if any, in the study as a whole, and those related to the individual elements, e.g., factors influencing cost, speed, productivity, and quality.
Forms/ Types	Find out the types of machinery being used, technology applied, etc.
Characteristics	Verify quality of machinery, attributes of methods, etc.
Comparisons	Establish how this process compares to other processes within the organization in terms of efficiency, cost-effectiveness, etc., and to similar processes in similar organizations (benchmarking) in terms of productivity, quality, etc.
Alternatives	Explore the available options or choices, or the possible courses of action across the elements, e.g., alternative cost controls, technology, methods, etc.
Constraints	Verify the prevailing restrictions, limitations, or controls in force, internal and external, e.g., speed of machines and financial resources (internal), legislation in force and supply of raw material (external).

The role of the Depths within the framework of the Ambit can be shown diagrammatically. Imagine that the issue or topic in question is a multi-angled physical object. The Ambit represents its frame or skeleton, while the Depths are the different specifics inside the object. This is illustrated in Figure 5.2.

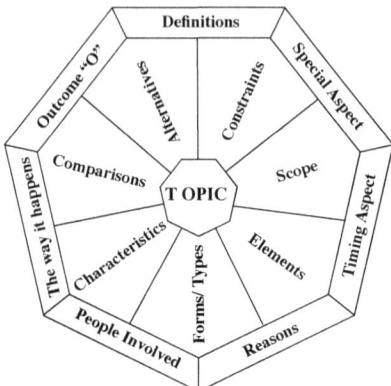

Figure 5.1
The Mangement Model

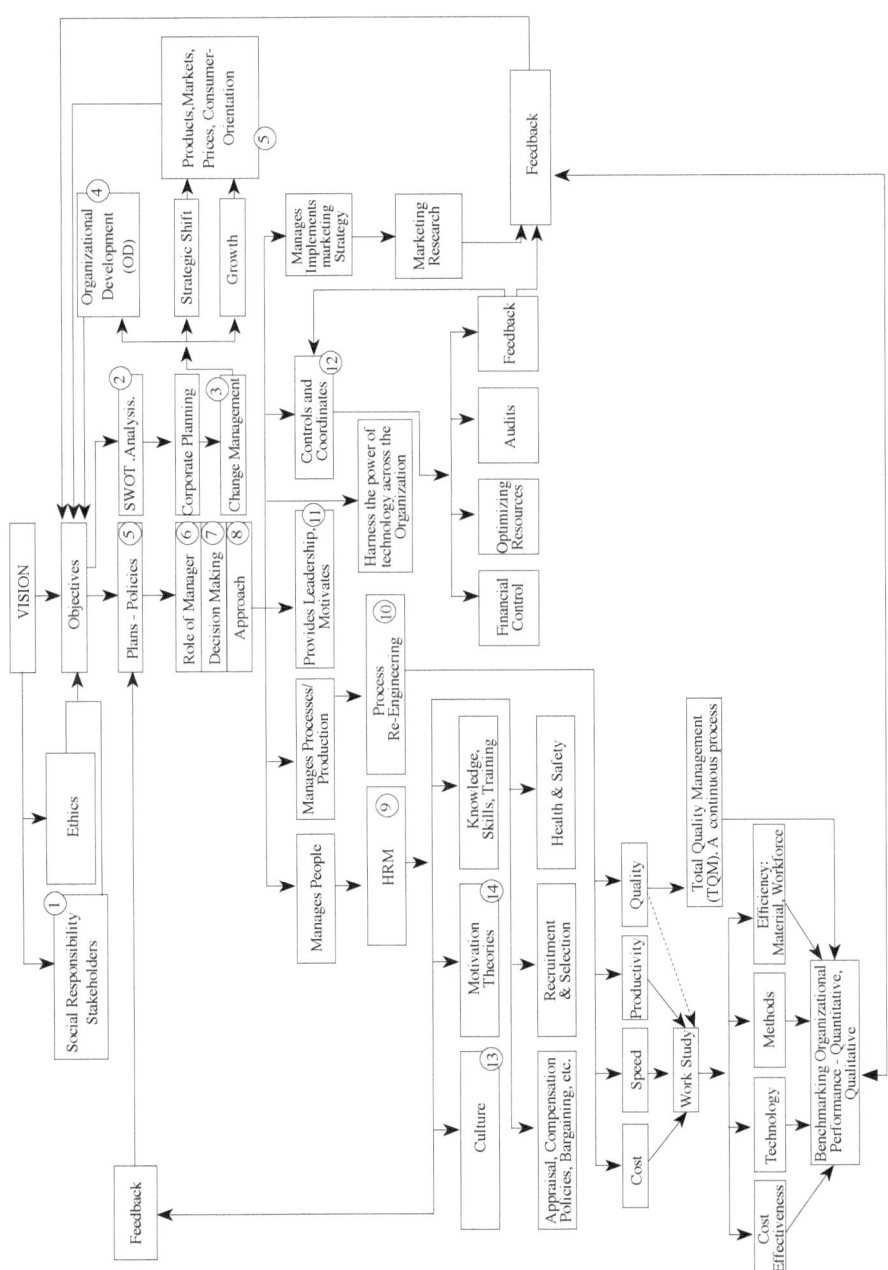

Key to the Management Model:

The following are brief explanations of the terms used in the numbered boxes in the Management Model.

1. Stakeholders: A term that refers to shareholders, customers, employees, and the community at large.
2. SWOT Analysis: Stands for the analysis of strengths, weaknesses, opportunities, and threats (of an organization).
3. Change Management: It can be at the operational or strategic/corporate levels, involving change in the overall direction of the organization. It is often done concurrently with an Organizational Development (OD) project.
4. Organizational Development (OD): Involves reviewing the mission and objectives; structure; job design; technology in use; work flow; markets; distribution channels; communication; and lines of command. It can be done at different levels according to the needs, e.g., at the corporate level for the entire organization or at the departmental/operational levels encompassing process re-engineering.
5. Marketing Mix: Comprised of product, price, promotion, and place (Distribution).
6. Role of Managers: They manage people; resources; activities; information; energy; projects; and quality, and ensure control.
7. Decision-Making Process: Involves defining the problem; gathering information; identifying alternative courses of action/solutions; assessing the pros and cons of each; selecting the optimum solution; implementing it; and assessing the outcomes.
8. Approaches to Management: They include Management by Exception, Management by Objectives (MBO), and Management by Walking Around.
9. Human Resources Management: Involves recruitment, compensation, industrial relations, compliance with legislation, training and development, and health and safety.
10. Process Re-engineering: Entails work study, work design, job design, work groups, reviewing organizational structure, and communication channels.
11. Leadership Types: They include charismatic, traditional, situational, appointed, functional, and principle-centered types.

12. Control: Entails setting of standards of performance, identifying variances/variations, and taking corrective action.
13. Culture: It is a product of policies, procedures, organizational structure, expertise, technology, communication channels, delegation of authority, and desired goals.
14. Motivation Theories: They include the Hawthorne Studies; Maslow's Hierarchy of Needs; McGregor's Theory X and Theory Y; Herzberg's Motivation-Hygiene Theory; Michigan Studies (Likert); Chris Argyris's Immaturity-Maturity Theory; McClelland's Achievement Motivation; Vroom's Expectancy Theory; Equity Theory (Kelly); Reinforcement Theory (Skinner); and The Japanese Theory Z.

Table 5.1
List of Key Words
Sorted by Relationship to the Management Model

Key Word/Phrase	Relation to Management Model	Relation to 6 Ws & O
Added Value	Cross - Topic Correlation	Outcome of, How Much
Alternatives (else)	Cross - Topic Correlation	All Ws & O
Assumptions	Cross - Topic Correlation	What is the Basis
Benchmarking	Organizational Performance	How others do it
Characteristics	Cross - Topic Correlation	How it performs/ looks like
Comparisons	Cross - Topic Correlation	All Ws & O
Competition	Products, Markets, etc.	Who else
Constraints	Cross - Topic Correlation	What are the limits
Control Change Management / Leadership	Controls and Coordinates Corporate Planning	All Ws & O All Ws & O
Cost	Manages Processes	How much
Critical/Creative Thinking	Role of Manager	All Ws & O
Customer, focus on	Products, Markets, etc.	Who to serve and How
Cycles	Manages Processes	When
Efficiency	Manages Processes	How effective
Elements of…	Cross - Topic Correlation	What is involved
Factors	Cross - Topic Correlation	What is involved

Key Word/Phrase	Relation to Management Model	Relation to 6 Ws & O
Forms of / Types of…	Cross - Topic Correlation	What is/are
Legislation/Rules	Cross - Topic Correlation	What is to abide by
Macro vs. Micro Level	SWOT Analysis	What is the scope
Market Share, Growth, Segments	Corporate Planning	Where, How much
Marketing Mix	Products, Markets, etc.	What is involved
Performance	Benchmarking/Controls & Coordinates	How efficient/effective
Productivity	Benchmarking	How much
Quality/Qualitative	TQM	How good
Quantity/Quantitative	Cross - Topic Correlation	How much
Risks	SWOT Analysis	What is involved
Safety and Health	Social responsibility	Who to protect and How
Scope	Cross - Topic Correlation	What are the limits of…
Short Term vs. Long Term	Plans, Policies	When
Sources	Cross - Topic Correlation	Where from
Speed	Manages Processes	How fast
Stakeholders	Social Responsibility	Who is concerned
SWOT Analysis	Policies	All Ws & O
Tasks	Process Re-engineering	What is being done
Technology	Harness the Power of Technology	What is being used
Total Quality Management	TQM	All Ws & O

Action Verbs:

Essay-type, open-ended questions often include an action verb that asks you to take a specific action with respect to the question. A question may ask you, for instance, to discuss, compare, or evaluate; it may ask you to describe, illustrate, or outline. There are many action verbs that you may encounter at essay exams. It is imperative to grasp these verbs and understand exactly what each of them means. Table 5.4 lists such verbs and the meaning of each.

Table 5.2
Action Verbs

Action Verb	Meaning
Advise	Give a recommendation; provide an opinion based on knowledge or expertise
Analyze	Explore, discuss and evaluate different aspects of the topic
Assess	Weigh up the significance of the idea, concept, or subject in question; argue its pros and cons
Compare	Explain how the ideas, concepts, or objects in question relate to each other in terms of similarities and differences
Contrast	Explain the disparities between ideas, concepts, or objects
Criticize	Give a substantiated opinion about the issue by assessing its merits or significance
Define	Give the specific meaning of a term, or description of something
Describe	Give a detailed explanation of something
Discuss	Provide your argument about the different aspects of a topic
Distinguish (between)	Identify the differences between the things in question
Enumerate	Itemize and explain the facets or elements of the issue
Examine	Scrutinize the topic, give a thorough account thereof
Evaluate	Carefully assess the topic and state your opinion and the basis thereof
Illustrate	Describe the issue and substantiate your statements or arguments
Interpret	Clarify the issue or its meaning; illuminate by comparisons and assessment
Outline	Give a summary of key points, ideas, concepts, etc.
Prove	Substantiate the argument by evidence or facts
Review	Go over the subject and evaluate its different aspects
State	Specifically explain the issue in question
Summarize	Provide a summary of the topic or issue, citing only key points, arguments, or conclusions
Trace	Identify chain of events, relationships between different things, or the roots/causes of something

Chapter 6

The Communication Process

Human communication is an area of study in its own right that has a significant impact on our lives. We continually communicate with family, friends, and neighbors; with peers, superiors, and customers; verbally, in writing, and in many other ways.

This chapter aims to provide a highlight on communication, including its definition, elements, and barriers.

The term communication has been defined in different ways. The following are examples:

According to Murphy and Peck (1987), "Communication is a process of transmitting a message so that the recipient understands it."

Baguley (1994) has defined it as, "The process by which information is passed between individuals and/or organizations by means of previously agreed symbols."

A sound communication skill is key to our success in the various domains of life. We need to transmit a correct and understandable message in a suitable form, through the appropriate channel or media, at the proper time, to the right person, in the particular place.

Elements of the Communication Process:

Different schools of thought have identified different elements of communication. Table 6.1 lists and describes the common elements.

Table 6.1
Summary of Elements of Communication

ELEMENT	DESCRIPTION
Sender	The person or party who initiates or sends the message
Message	An idea, subject matter, information, prompt, etc. initiated by the sender
Channel	The medium through which the message is transmitted, e.g., e-mail, publication, broadcasting, etc
Receiver	The person or party who ultimately receives the message
Transmission	The process of sending the message through the particular channel
Encoding	The process of originating/composing the message, using appropriate codes or language, in a way that should make the message understandable by the receiver
Decoding	The process of interpreting the meaning of the message by the receiver
Meaning	The aim, intention, or implication of the message as intended by the sender or perceived by the receiver
Feedback	The response sent by the receiver to the sender of the original message, followed by a further response by the latter to the former
Communication Effects	The results or consequences of the messages exchanged at the two sides of the process, i.e., by the sender and the receiver

Communication Barriers:

There are barriers or difficulties that, if they prevail, may hamper the communication process and distort the message. Similar to the elements of the communication process, different works have identified different communication barriers.

A summary of communication barriers discussed by different works is depicted in Table 6.2

Table 6.2
Summary of Communication Barriers

Barrier	Meaning/Manifestation	Remedy
Lack of Proper Communication Skills	Inability to communicate effectively – verbally or in writing; manifested by: - Being unsure about what to communicate and how - Composing or delivering ambiguous, incomplete, or negative message - Choosing inappropriate channel, language, or form of communication	Proper education, training, and practice in the communication skills
Perceptions of Reality	The conclusions, presumptions and judgments that communicators make based on their background, value-system or fixations; manifested by: - Stereotyping or faulty generalizations: judging a whole (like a group of people) based on the communicator's perception about a part of it - Making faulty inferences, judgments, or evaluations before or without knowing the facts - The «Allness Fallacy»: stating or implying that something is true of an entire class of things	Positive attitudes, rational thinking, and openness toward others; enlightenment

Barrier	Meaning/Manifestation	Remedy
Attitudes, Opinions and Emotions	Include anger, hatred, and fear (of the consequences of the message), and lack of trust; manifested by communicating in a rough and aggressive way; unfair treatment of certain groups of people; hiding information; and deception. It is a complex barrier, as it relates to cultivation and refinement.	A healthy atmosphere that fosters trust, teamwork, and tolerance; counseling; education
Status Differences	Subordinates refrain from communicating with, or passing information to their superiors to avoid criticism or irresponsiveness.	Receptiveness on the part of superiors; encouraging communication; appropriate communication channels
Information Overload	Often results from organizational defects, inappropriate/unclear communication channels, and/or a poorly designed information management system It is manifested by dispatching too much messages or providing too much information in a way that disrupts work.	Proper organizational structure; clear channels; proper information systems
Message Distortion "Chinese whisper"	Prevails when a message is transmitted through a series of people; each one adds or deletes from it for different reasons, e.g. misunderstanding the message, or deliberate distortion because of the receiver's attitudes or feelings toward the message.	Original message should be clear, short, and easily understandable; avoid excessive details, jargon, and ambiguity.

Barrier	Meaning/Manifestation	Remedy
Environmental Problems	Include: - Noise - Technical problems (e.g. system failure) - Lack of channels (like meetings, telephones, etc) - Distance	- Quiet environment - Proper equipment - Appropriate channels - Modern technology, e.g. e-mail, telephone, etc.
Interpretation of Words	Misinterpretation of words takes place when the words or symbols used to communicate have different meanings in the minds of the sender and receiver according to their backgrounds and knowledge	Avoid jargon; use common language wherever possible; ensure message is understood; get feedback.

Understanding the role of communication elements and barriers is of paramount significance for the creation of a meaningful content. We need to focus on the receiver, in this case the examiner, to fulfill his/her needs. At the exam, avoid barriers like information overload or the allness fallacy; be direct and to the point; write clearly; use words that cannot be misinterpreted; avoid generalizations and substantiate your views or arguments.

Chapter 7
Business Writing

Writing an exam is a communication process. You endeavor to express your ideas in a way that convinces examiners of your knowledge and ability. Your answer can be more effective if you keep in mind certain considerations.

This chapter briefly discusses the important considerations in the process of Business Writing in general. Any writing activity requires knowledge of the topic to be addressed and should have clear objectives and purpose. It requires proper planning, sound writing skills, appropriate style, and suitable structure of the content.

Elements of Writing:

According to Baguley (1994), writing entails four elements:

Planning: The process of defining the purpose of the content, deciding on research techniques and content, and choosing appropriate style and presentation.

Generating text: The complex process of writing the text. It requires knowledge of the topic in question and involves various tasks and considerations. These include developing ideas, constructing sentences, and organizing them logically according to the plan. Using the Ambit and Depths in this technique shall help in dealing with numerous topics and determining the aspects relevant to them. Other considerations include observing correct grammar, spelling and usage of words.

Revising: The process of adding, deleting, or reorganizing ideas and sentences; of revising the plans, goals, and structure; and of checking grammar, spelling, usage of words, etc.

Style: It "is a distinctive manner of expression" (Merriam-Webster's 2003). It is an important factor that determines the effectiveness of the content and influences the impact of the message on the receivers. A style can be formal or informal, specialized or lay, general or particular, determinate or indeterminate. It can also be complex or simple, practical or emotional, reasoned or exhortative.

Principles of Business Writing:

An effective content helps you reach your audience and make the desired impact. You may rightly ask, "What makes an effective content?" Murphy and Peck (1987) recommend applying the Seven Cs of effective communication. These are briefly described as follows:

1. Completeness: Cover all aspects of the topic. To this end, utilize the Ambit in addition to the Management Model, Key Words, and the Practical Lexicon.
2. Conciseness: Organize appropriately, provide relevant facts, and avoid repetition. Be straight to the point.
3. Consideration: Focus on "you" instead of "I" and "we"; show interest in reader/audience and emphasize positive and pleasant facts with integrity.
4. Concreteness: Give specific data; choose clear words and action verbs to build images in the audience's minds.
5. Clarity: Use familiar words, short sentences, and paragraphs. Include examples, illustrations, and other visual aids, such as charts or graphs, if applicable.
6. Courtesy: Be tactful, thoughtful, and appreciative. Avoid negative expressions. Respond promptly and good-naturedly.
7. Correctness: Include only accurate facts, figures, and correct words. Choose nonsexist expressions. Use the correct level of language.

The Seven Cs can be illustrated diagrammatically as shown in Figure 7.1.

Figure 7.1
The Seven Cs

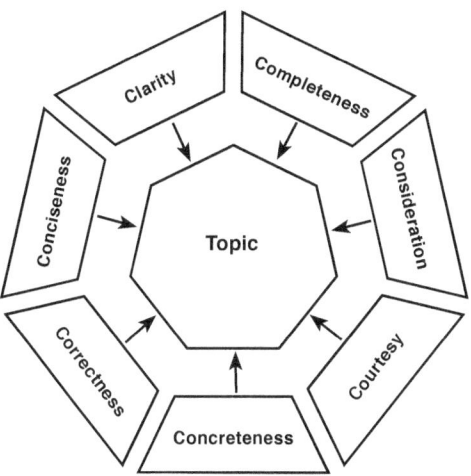

Chapter 8

The Examination Technique

Chapter 1 briefly discussed the challenges that students face at the examination hall. These challenges include:
1. Organization: To tackle an exam paper in an organized manner within a given time
2. Main Points: To recall and determine the main points, ideas, or arguments to be addressed or covered
3. Recalling Facts: To associate the main points generated in (2) above with other points to trigger more ideas or arguments
4. Style: To adopt an appropriate style, proper grammar, and correct spelling and punctuation
5. Vocabulary: To elaborate on each point, idea, or argument in an orderly manner, using appropriate vocabulary.

Impressive works on management (Cole 2004) have given various recommendations to establish an Examination Technique, a term that is widely used to denote the recommended steps and time management techniques through which students can tackle examination papers in a more effective manner.

The following steps are a recap of such recommendations and constitute a typical examination technique:
1. Read the instructions on the examination sheet carefully and ascertain what is required
2. See how many questions you must answer
3. Read the questions quickly, and tick the ones you are sure you can answer, even if they are less than the required number

4. If some questions have sub-questions, tick the ones that have more sub-questions that you can answer
5. If you ticked more questions than required, review the questions, their sub-questions, and their marks. Select the questions that can potentially earn you more marks
6. Allocate appropriate time for each question
7. Select the easiest question and read it carefully Determine explicit and implicit points and issues and sub-questions within it
8. Make a list of key points, arrange them in a logical order, and start writing your answer accordingly
9. Answer the other selected questions in the same manner
10. Watch the time; try your best to stick to the time assigned for each question
11. When you have answered a few questions, check the time again. See how many more questions you must answer. Reallocate the time. Save a few minutes for the end.
12. In case you run short of time and there is still a question or more to answer, close the question you are working on and start on the remaining one(s). Write the key points or main arguments and give a brief explanation on each
13. Check the numbering and sequence of the answer sheets
14. Utilize the remaining few minutes, if any, in revising and adding to your answers, especially the last short ones.

The above recommendations are concerned with the technique by which you may approach an examination paper in a more systematic manner and manage the allotted time. However, as stated before, none of the concepts, techniques, or processes discussed in this part of the book can alone address all the challenges of writing. This includes the Examination Technique. Alone, it can only be a useful time management tool. However, it does not help students with determining main points, recalling facts, vocabulary, and style, though it recommends them to do so.

Students can address these challenges with the help of the Ambit Technique's components, i.e., the 6 Ws & O, the Management Model, Key Words, etc. As such, the examination technique has been adapted and merged with other components to create the Ambit Technique that is described in the next part.

Part Three
Utilizing the Ambit Technique

Introduction

In the previous two parts of the book, we have discussed the challenges of writing, the background research, as well as the different components of the Ambit Technique and the roles that each one plays within it. We have made our case as to why this technique is needed, what purposes it serves, and the help it provides.

This part is concerned with utilizing the Ambit Technique. It is divided into two chapters. The first chapter summarizes the various issues involved and the preparations required prior to using the technique. The second chapter takes you step by step toward using the Ambit Technique, and includes a corresponding flowchart.

Chapter 9

The Ambit Technique Recap

The Ambit Technique is a tool that helps with tackling essay-type, open-ended exam questions in the management fields, as well as written material at the workplace. It aims to help you recall relevant points or issues, and trigger ideas and arguments that you should have already studied and are aware of. It is by no means a substitute for knowledge and proper preparation. Students often encounter questions that involve specific definitions, facts, numbers, etc. Knowledge and thorough study are required to address such questions.

Appreciation of the following concepts is vital for a successful application of the technique:

1. The Communication Process
2. The Concept of Association

The significance of the Communication Process cannot be overemphasized. Understanding its elements and barriers is pivotal for any form of communication, verbal or in writing. Central to the Communication Process are the receivers. Their needs, background, and perceived expectations, in addition to the nature of the topic, are determining factors in the choice of language, style, amount of detail, etc.

The Concept of Association acts as a mechanism in the mind and the inner self that helps you to retrieve the desired information or knowledge.

Once you have understood the concepts and roles of its components, you shall be able to benefit from the Ambit Technique without further instruction. You can particularly benefit from the use of the Ambit and Depths in conjunction with the Management Model and the Key Words, in addition to the Practical Lexicon. The technique has been supported by a flowchart (Figure 10.1)

To summarize the relevance of each of the components of the Ambit Technique to the needs of students, Table 9.1 illustrates the relationship of each component to each of the challenges of writing that they encounter.

Table 9.1

Challenges of Students:

Challenge	Related Component
Organization	The Examination Technique
Main points	The Management Model and Key Words
Recalling facts	The Concept of Association and the 6 Ws & O
Vocabulary	The Practical Lexicon
Style	Business Writing

Further, it shall be very helpful for students to practice the Ambit Technique before attempting exams. That shall help them memorize the Management Model and Key Words, which is essential. On the other hand, reviewing the Practical Lexicon repetitively shall also help students to be acquainted with it in a way closer to complete memorization. All that shall prepare students to effectively use the Ambit Technique under examination conditions.

In the process that follows, it shall be assumed that the students have done their homework and that these concepts have been understood and are embraced in the ways shown earlier. You will notice during the process that the step involving the use of the Ambit and Depths in conjunction with the Key Words may need to be used repetitively each time a new issue, point, or argument is addressed. That shall help trigger more ideas within each individual context.

As for the timing, utilizing the Ambit Technique shall obviously take several extra minutes, but it is a good time investment. It shall save considerable time during the process of planning, organizing, and writing of the material. This is because the Ambit Technique shall help you identify the key points, or most of them, as well as sub-points, which will culminate in a tentative plan and structure of the text. Subsequently, the task of writing the material shall be easier and less time consuming.

Once you have determined the main headings and subheadings, you shall be more confident and organized, and shall spend less time in elaboration. As such, you can ultimately achieve better results.

Chapter 10

The Process: Utilizing the Ambit Technique At the Exam

The following steps describe the process of utilizing the Ambit Technique. Please read these steps carefully and then study the corresponding flowchart in Figure 10.1.

1. Remember the receiver, i.e., an examiner who wants to test your knowledge. The message is your answer. The channel is your answer sheet. Your answer (message) should be meaningful and comprehensible. Make sure that it achieves its objective, i.e., convincing the examiner of your mastery of the subject. Remember that you have no chance for feedback. The examiner shall not, and cannot, come back to you for verification. The only feedback you can get will be your grade mark.
2. Read the instructions carefully and ascertain what is required. Focus on the "Action Verb," if any, e.g. discuss, outline, or describe (Table 5.4).

    a - Ascertain the number of questions you must answer.

    b - Read the questions quickly and tick the ones you are sure you can answer, even if they are less than the required number.

    c - If some questions have sub-questions, tick the ones that have more sub-questions that you can answer.

    d - If you ticked more questions than the number required, review the questions, their sub-questions, and their marks. Select the ones that can potentially earn you more marks.

    e - Be confident. Unleash your power and influence. You have at your disposal an effective tool that gives you an advantage.

f - Allocate appropriate time for each question. Save few minutes for the end.
3. Select the easiest question and read it carefully. Determine explicit and implicit points and issues, keeping in mind the action verbs.
   a - Determine the number of sub-questions within it.
   b - Determine its Ambit. Make a list of the key points that come to your mind. Focus on action verbs.
   c - Recall the Management Model. Try to relate the question to one or more of its headings.
   d - Start using the Ambit and Depths in conjunction with the Key Words (memorizing them is essential). Try to associate the culminated points with other concepts, issues, or topics.
   e - Note down all key points that come to your mind. Then look at the question again and make a quick cross-checking of the key points. Eliminate unnecessary or overlapping ones.
   f - Arrange the points appropriately in logical sequence. Decide on headings and subheadings as the case may be.
   g - Answer the questions in the sequence required (if any).
   h - Write confidently and clearly. Substantiate your arguments.
   i - Keep to the point. Avoid out- of -context issues. Be careful of grammar, spelling, and punctuation, and write clearly.
   j - Further relevant key points might come to your mind while writing. Add them to the list.
   k - Watch the time allotted to the question. Try your best to stick to it.
   l - Revise your answer and make necessary alterations.
4. Answer the other selected questions in the same manner as in (3) above. Leave a few lines between answers for further additions at the end.
5. Check how many more questions you should answer. Check and reallocate the time. Save a few minutes for the end.
   a - Now that you have answered a few questions, you have gained more confidence and have trained your mind. When you look at the remaining questions again, you will feel more confident of making a better choice than at the beginning. Look at the remaining questions to choose from them. Take the first one. Quickly review in your mind the Management Model and Key Words. Note down the points that come to your mind. Quickly try to associate the key points with other

relevant concepts, issues, or topics. Note down whatever comes to your mind.

b - If you feel confident, start answering the question as in (3) above. Otherwise, repeat the process (5a) on another question, then the next.

c - Make sure you have answered, or attempted, the required number of questions.

6. Check the time.

   a - In case you run short of time and there is still a question or more to answer, close the question you are working on, and start on the remaining one(s). Write the key points and give a brief explanation on each (this may earn you more marks).

   b - Check the time again while working. Reserve two minutes for the final step.

7. Utilize the remaining time (if any) to add any further relevant points to your answers.

At the end of the exam, use the reserved two minutes to make sure that your answer sheets are correctly numbered and collated and that your name, number, etc. are clearly written.

Figure 10.1

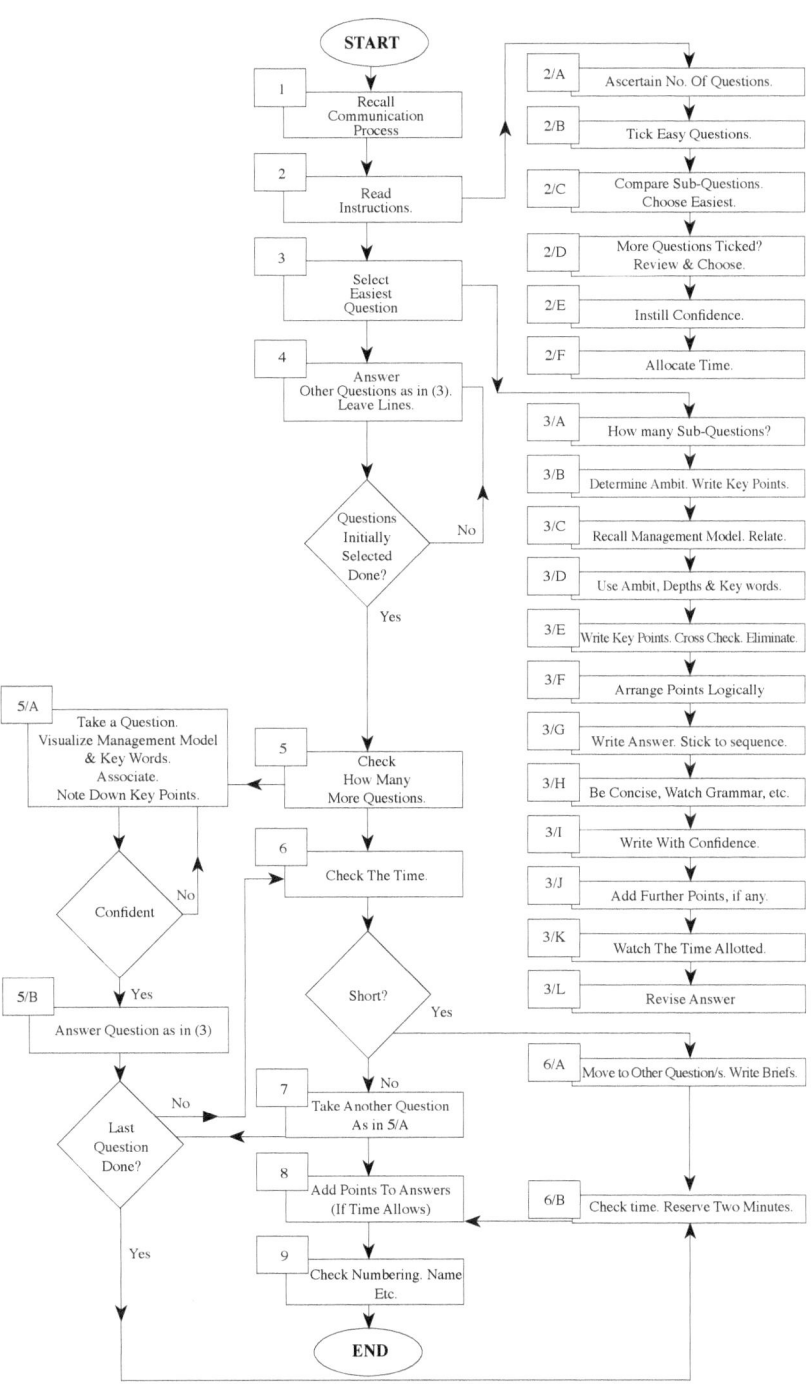

Part Four

The Practical Lexicon for Business Management

Introduction

The Practical Lexicon is not intended to include every word or term you may find in management dictionaries. It rather aims to provide a concise and usable list of management terms that are essential in the context of most examinations and written materials in the workplace.

In general, the list can be distinguished from most management dictionaries in that it excludes the following:

1. The obvious and widely known words, e.g., bank, bank account, etc.
2. The phrases that are formed in the normal way words are used, e.g., Absence of Demand.
3. The rarely used words and terms.

It is worth noting that no one list can accommodate all the needs of all readers. However, care has been taken to ensure that the list substantially covers a wide spectrum of business topics.

The list is chiefly sorted in alphabetical order. However, discretion has been used to tailor it to the needs of students and professionals in the best possible way.

To this end, terms that are derivatives of particular terms, or closely related to particular topics have been listed under that term or topic regardless of their alphabetical order. Under the term "Accounting," for example, Financial Accounting and Management Accounting have been listed. In addition, other terms that do not include the word *accounting*, but nevertheless are directly related to it, have also been listed, such as Financial Management and Cash Flow. Under the term Human Resources Management (HRM), related concepts, procedures, and issues have been listed as well. Terms, which are general, and can be useful in several contexts, have been listed according to their alphabetical order.

Therefore, in order to make the best possible use of the list, the following is recommended:

1. Go through the list several times to familiarize yourself with the way words are listed and the logic behind it.
2. When you study a particular topic, go directly to the main terms, e.g., Accounting, HRM, etc. Should you need the meaning of further words that are not listed under the particular topic, you may search for them according to their alphabetical order.
3. In case you are writing on a topic, or going to sit for a particular exam, go to the main terms under that topic and study them thoroughly. Then go through the rest of the list to identify any other words or terms that might be useful for the topic at hand.

Chapter 11
The Lexicon

A

Accounting The systematic recording of a business' financial transactions according to approved principles and standards, and summarizing them into reports and statements that reflect the financial status of a business at a given date and its performance during an accounting period.

- **Financial Accounting** Aimed at reporting to shareholders on the overall performance of their company. Reports are mainly produced in the form of Profit and Loss Accounts and Balance Sheets.
- **Cost Accounting** A branch of Management Accounting concerned with determining or, at times, estimating the cost of units of production, a process, etc. It entails identifying the pertinent cost components, e.g., material, labor, overheads, etc., and determining or estimating the monetary value of each.
- **Financial Management** A branch of management which is concerned with the overall planning and control of a firm's financial operations. It aims at obtaining and utilizing a firm's funds in the best profitable manner.
- **Management Accounting** Aimed at producing detailed information to the Management of a business to help them make informed decisions on planning and controlling its various operations.
- **Accounting Ratio** A way of establishing the relationship between accounting figures by placing a figure as a ratio or percentage of another.

- **Accounting Standards** Principles aimed at streamlining the accounting treatment of the numbers that are stated in a firm's books of accounts, in order to ensure consistency in reporting profits and losses.
- **Cash Flow** The movement of cash in and out of a firm. The former takes the form of sales receipts and other sources of income, while the latter results from payments for materials and other types of expenses.
- **Allocation** An accounting process whereby costs and revenues are distributed in some agreeable manner between the various products, processes, departments, units, etc.

Accruals Expenses that have been incurred but not yet paid and that need to be included in the accounting results of a trading or fiscal period.

Accumulated fund Denotes the capital and retained earnings that a non-profit organization has accumulated over the years.

Acquittance A written clearance stating that a debt or any other form of financial liability or obligation has been fulfilled or fully paid.

Activity level The production capacity of a business, production unit, etc., measured in terms of quantity of production or the resources available, i.e., labor hours, machine hours, machine production capacity, etc.

Advertising Conveying to buyers through media and other channels the nature and characteristics of a product/brand and urging them to buy it in order for a firm to increase sales.
- **Advertising Effectiveness Test** A measure of the actual, or estimation of the anticipated effects of advertising on the sales of a firm's products.
- **Advertising Platform** The most convincing feature of a product which is relevant to the needs of the targeted consumers.
- **Advocacy Advertising** An advertising approach aimed at fostering, on the part of the audience, a certain belief or course of action.

Agenda A list of points or issues planned for discussion at a meeting.

Agent An intermediary employed by a person, group of persons, or a firm to arrange a contract between them and a third party.

Allotment The allocation of newly-issued shares to prospective shareholders.

Allowance
- In calculating a standard time for carrying out a task, an additional time (allowance) is accounted for to cater for human needs and operational unforeseen circumstances.
- An additional payment made to an employee as compensation for certain

inconvenience or hazard, e.g., Shift Allowance.
- Additional material or components intended to cater for losses, wastage, etc. and that are included in the quantity of material, components, etc. (called basic material) required for manufacturing a product.
- Tax allowances, or relief, made available by the tax authorities to individuals whose income falls below certain brackets and to companies who invest in new plants and machinery, computers, etc. (Capital Allowance)

Amalgamation A form of external growth (see Growth) whereby a group of firms, in the same or different industries, agree to merge together to form one larger business entity and pool their resources in order to gain such benefits as reduction of costs, increased market share, etc. The alternative term Merger is also used to denote the same process.

Analysis The critical and careful examination of the different aspects or details of something.
- **Breakeven Analysis** An examination of the data pertinent to fixed costs, variable costs, selling price, etc. in order to determine the level of sales at which the company recovers both fixed and variable costs, making neither profit nor loss.
- **Cause and Effect Analysis** The process of identifying and examining the causes of production defects in order to act appropriately to avoid them.
- **Cost-Benefit Analysis** The study of the anticipated advantages and disadvantages of a proposed project, mainly from a social viewpoint.
- **Critical Path Analysis** A technique used to identify the shortest way of completing projects that involve different activities. A network of arrows is drawn to illustrate the interrelationship of the activities. It shows the activities that can be carried out simultaneously, those dependent on others, and those critical to the completion of the project.
- **Customer Analysis** A study aimed to identify and segment the customers of a business, their preferences, values, and the choices they have.
- **Gap Analysis** A term used in various contexts to denote the analysis of the difference between an expectation or requirement on the one hand, and the actual achievement on another. Examples are (1) the difference between job requirements and the skills of the job incumbent, (2) the difference between customers' expectations and the quality

of merchandise produced or the services provided (3) the difference between the goals of a business and what it has actually achieved.
- **Organizational Analysis** The examination of organizational structures, job designs, lines of command, spans of control, and distribution of authority for decision-making.
- **Ratio Analysis** An accounting technique that aims at analyzing various aspects of the business, e.g., liquidity, profitability, and other performance measures by using accounting ratios (see "Accounting Ratios"). It can also be used to compare the performance of a business with that of comparable ones.
- **Regression Analysis** A statistical method used for forecasting the value of unknown variables, which are dependent on other known and independent variables, by generating the causal relationship between them.
- **Sensitivity Analysis** A way of setting different scenarios for evaluating a project whereby hypothetical changes in the underlying assumptions are considered to evaluate their likely impacts on the project's outcomes, rate of return, etc., with the ultimate objective of assessing the sensitivity of the project's profitability to such changes.
- **SWOT Analysis** A basis for formulating a firm's strategies. It involves pinpointing the firm's internal strengths (S) and weaknesses (W), the external opportunities (O) it can exploit, and the threats (T) that challenge it.
- **System Analysis** A speciality within Information Technology whereby a Systems Analyst analyzes an operation or process and transforms it into flowcharts according to which a computer programmer may write a program to automate that operation or process.
- **Workflow Analysis** An aspect of job analysis whereby the flow of work across the various jobs in focus is recorded and examined. The purpose is to establish whether a particular job or jobs need to be designed in a more practical, satisfying, or productive manner.
- **Variance Analysis** The examination of the differences between actual and standard (budgeted) costs, output, or revenues. Variances include machine hour variance, overhead cost variance, material cost variance, labor cost variance, sales revenue variance, and total cost variance.

Annuity Uniform amounts of money paid at predetermined intervals to an investor as an interest on a fixed investment, or to an insured person or her/his heirs against an insurance policy.

Antitrust Legislation A law aiming at restricting monopolistic practices of businesses and ensuring free competition.

Apportionment Certain cost components cannot be allocated accurately to individual departments, units, processes, etc. Alternatively, they are shared out between those in a rational manner, e.g., per meter square, machine hours, etc. In some cases, certain revenues are treated similarly.

Articles of association The charter of a joint-stock company that regulates the relationship between the company and its shareholders.

Assets Items that have values, e.g., land, property, machinery, cash, etc., and that are owned by an individual or an entity like a company, organization, etc. They fall into two main categories, Fixed Assets and Current Assets, although sometimes are categorized as Intangible Assets, Financial Assets, and Physical Assets.

- **Fixed Assets** Intended for long-term use, e.g., plants, machinery, land, buildings, etc. (see Depreciation)
- **Current Assets** Intended for short-term use, e.g., cash, stocks, bank deposits, debtors, etc.
- **Physical Assets** Include land, buildings, plants, machinery, etc. (Fixed Assets in nature).
- **Financial Assets** Include cash, shares, deposits, etc. (Current Assets).
- **Intangible Assets** Nonmaterial assets, like brands and goodwill (Fixed Assets in most cases).
- **Net Assets** The total of a firm's Net Current Assets (Current Assets less Current Liabilities) and Fixed Assets.
- **Net Current Assets** Represents the difference between a firm's Current Assets and its Current Liabilities, and constitutes the working capital of a firm.
- **Total Assets** The total of a firm's Current Assets (including Current Liabilities) and Fixed Assets.
- **Assets Turnover** A calculation that examines the degree to which a firm's assets are efficiently utilized. It denotes the sales revenues of a firm as a percentage of its Total Assets.
- **Asset Structure** The manner in which a firm's assets are comprised. The monetary value of each type of asset, i.g., Fixed and Current Assets are

depicted in the Balance Sheet as a ratio of the total value of assets.

Auction A method whereby buyers compete to procure goods or services which are sold to the bidder who offers the highest price.

Audit An inspection of the account books of a firm, organization, etc. to ensure their accuracy, or a review of its operations, processes, etc. to ensure their efficiency and compliance with internal and external policies or regulations. Audit types include financial, operational, technical, and management audits.

Automation The utilization of machinery, computers, etc. for carrying out standardized or repetitive operations, processes, or tasks to speed up operations, increase efficiency, and reduce manpower costs.

Average The mean value of a number of values. It can be calculated by adding up a series of values and then dividing the total by the number of values which were added up.

- **Weighted Average** A means of calculating an average for a number of values where some values are assigned or bear more weight than others do.

B

Backlog The overall quantity or the number of unfulfilled orders of a firm at a given point of time.

Balance Sheet A statement of accounts that lists the assets and liabilities of a firm, and the value of each, at the end of an accounting period.

Bank Reconciliation A procedure whereby individuals or firms match up their records of cash receipts and payments with those shown in the bank statements.

Behavioural Science Concerned with the study of people at work, their behavioural patterns, motivation, performance, etc., against factors such as work environment, company policies, communication channels, nature of work, etc. (see Organizational Behaviour)

Benchmarking The process of examining and adopting the best practices of competitors in order for a firm to stand at equal or even better competitive footings.

Bond An instrument of borrowing long-term funds, which is issued by a government, firm, etc. at a fixed nominal value and a fixed interest rate and is repayable on maturity.

Bottleneck A pause, delay or time lag at a certain point or stage of an operation, process, etc. that interrupts the overall sequence of operations.

Bottom line The net profit of a firm.

Brainstorming An unconventional way of creating ideas by encouraging creative thinking. It is used to find solutions to difficult problems whereby the concerned staff, task force, etc. state their ideas as they occur and have them listed. Then the listed ideas are filtered and short-listed. The chosen ideas are discussed in depth to select the most viable one.

Branding A way of establishing brand loyalty on the part of consumers through extensive advertising and promotions to foster the consumers' ability to recognize the product's brand, and by ensuring the quality of product after sale services, etc.

Broker An intermediary (middle person) who brings together sellers and buyers of a product or service.

Bubble A hollow economy or business that bears a high risk and that creates growth rates that exceed the capabilities of the actual assets owned.

Budget The financial plan of an entity for a given period, usually a fiscal year. It shows the forecasted expenditures, sales revenues, other revenues, and the expected profits.

- **Budget Control** A system that constitutes a significant aspect of management accounting whereby the costs and revenues of a firm, organization, etc. are closely monitored and controlled. It entails comparing actual expenditures and revenues against budgets and taking corrective action as and when required.
- **Flexible Budget (or Variable Budget)** A budget that varies according to the level of activity. According to it, anticipated costs (and revenues) are linked to the level of output achieved. It constitutes grounds for establishing anticipated costs at different levels of output.
- **Functional Budget** A budgetary system that is designed according to the functions of an organization, whereby a budget is calculated for each function.
- **Rolling Budget** A budget that is updated continuously to accommodate contingencies and changes which are external in nature and fall beyond the control of the organization.
- **Zero-based Budgeting** A budgetary system whereby the budget of each function, department, etc. is assumed to be zero. Subsequently, each cost

component needs to be justified before inclusion to the budget.

Business Cycle The rise and fall of the aggregate business activity as a result of changes in circumstances, like supply and demand, influx and departure of investments, etc. The cycle goes in four stages: depression, recovery, boom, and recession, which leads to depression again.

Business objectives The goals that a business determines to accomplish in terms of profit, market share, growth, etc. It is part of the strategic planning of the business (see Management Model). Once a business sets its vision, it determines its objectives and then formulates detailed plans to achieve those objectives.

Business Process Re-engineering The systematic investigation of the various processes and operations within an organization in order to improve its efficiency. Modern approaches to this system emphasize an inter-departmental and multi-functional review of operations.

C

Capacity The highest quantity of production that the various assets of a firm, i.e., plant, machinery, labor, etc., can generate efficiently and cost-effectively.

Capital The amount of money invested to start a business. It is mainly utilized to procure the necessary assets.

- **Called-up Capital** The amount of money payable by shareholders upon allotment of shares to them.
- **Capital Allowances** (see Allowance)
- **Capital Appreciation** The rise in the value of an asset due to reasons such as inflation, surging land prices in certain areas (for land and properties), etc.
- **Capital Gain** The extra amount of money gained upon selling an asset for an amount higher than its original price.
- **Capital Gearing** A measure that shows the degree to which a firm's capital is geared by debts as opposed to shares. It is depicted by the ratio of long-term loans, or loan capital, to share capital.
- **Capital Intensiveness** A measure of the amount of capital equipment used by a firm in generating its products.
- **Capital Goods** Refers to Fixed Assets like plants, machinery, equipment, etc. that are used to generate products. In microeconomics, they are confined to a firm, whereas in macroeconomics, they denote the aggregate

amount of such items in the whole country or economy.
- **Net Current Assets** (see Assets)

Cartel Prohibited by law, it is an arrangement between assemblies of suppliers aimed at restraining competition between them (see Antitrust Regulation). According to it, the suppliers involved conspire to set uniformed prices for their products (and sometimes agree on production quotas). Thus, they create an ability to secure monopoly prices (see Monopoly).

Communication The exchange of information, thoughts, views, or feelings between people, organizations or organisms.

Company A business organization engaged in producing and/or selling commodities or services.
- **Public Limited Company** A type of joint-stock company that is financed by issuing shares to the public and which enjoys the status of an autonomous legal entity. Under this arrangement, the maximum loss to shareholders in case of the company's failure is limited by the amount they invested as shares in the company.
- **Private Limited Company** A joint-stock company with a limited number of shareholders and where the shares are not tradable in the stock exchange. However, it is protected by provisions made for limited liability companies.
- **Holding Company** A joint-stock company that owns more than 50 percent and up to 100 percent of the shares of another company or group of companies (called subsidiary companies), by virtue of which it gains control of the policies and affairs of these companies.
- **Subsidiary Company** A joint-stock company in which a holding company owns more than 50 percent and up to 100 percent of its voting shares. Thereby, the holding company owns it wholly or overwhelmingly, and gains control over its policies and affairs.
- **Associated Company** A joint-stock company in which a holding company owns a shareholding equivalent to 20 percent or more, but not exceeding 50 percent of its shares.
- **Sole Proprietorship** A business undertaking that is owned entirely by one person.

Competition The struggle among sellers of a commodity or service to retain their customers and gain new ones. Sellers incur significant costs in advertising and marketing campaigns. They improve quality of products and

reduce prices in order to secure a greater market share. (see Advertising, Market, and Pricing)
- **Competitive Advantage** The benefits that a firm has over its rivals. It culminates from having the right assets, raw material, distinguished brand names, etc., or from using advanced technology or huge machinery that gives economies of scale, or from capitalizing on its accumulated experience and innovation in the field.
- **Competitive Strategy** Part of the strategic plan of the business. It entails studying various factors, both internal to the firm (e.g., Technology, methods used, etc.) and external (e.g., markets, competition, customers, etc.), in order to create a situation whereby the business beats competitors and gains a competitive advantage.

Consortium A number of businesses pooling their resources in some agreeable manner to undertake a new business project.

Consumer Orientation A strategy according to which a business identifies its customers, their characteristics, needs, expectations, etc., and then designs and produces goods or services to fulfill them.

Copyright Property rights of authors, musicians, artists, etc. that give them ownership of intellectual works that they have produced and which are protected by law against unauthorized sale, reproduction, etc.

Core Business An organizational unit within a firm that is vital for the accomplishment of its goals. It encompasses the main line of the business and is the main source of its revenues.

Corporate Identity The attributes that characterize and distinguish an organization. These include the principles of the organization, its ethics, culture, goals, etc. A specially-designed logo is usually used by an organization to symbolize its identity.

Corporate Restructuring A strategic rearrangement of a business, which entails changes in the organizational structure and/or a strategic shift in the course and aims of the business as a whole.

Corporation A joint-stock company. (see Company)

Costing A system of identifying the costs of producing a firm's goods or services with the objective of determining selling prices of products, maintaining control over operations, or as an aid for informed decision-making. There are different factors that influence the costs of running a business. These include the size of the business; organization and efficiency of operations; the methods and technology in use; costs of logistics, material, and components; calibre of personnel; etc. (see Economy of Scale and Economy of Scope)

- **Absorption Costing** A method of costing whereby direct costs (direct material and direct labour) as well as overheads (indirect costs) are allocated to the individual units of production to arrive at the total cost per unit. An overhead cost per unit is calculated by dividing total overheads by the number of units produced.
- **Activity-Based Costing** A costing method that can be appropriate for highly automated processes. It concentrates on the total cost of running the business as a whole and the factors that determine such costs. Thus, it eliminates the distinction made by other costing methods between fixed and variable costs.
- **Cost Advantage Strategy** A strategy that aims at reducing costs below those of competitors without compromising quality, in order to gain competitive advantage.
- **Cost Center** An organizational unit within a firm, a function, or process, the costs of which can be identified for accounting purposes.
- **Cost Control** The process of monitoring costs in an organization whereby actual costs are compared against budgeted costs and variations, if any, are analyzed in detail to facilitate corrective action.
- **Cost of Capital** The weighted average cost of the different sources of long-term finances of a business, i.e., interest rates payable to the lending banks.
- **Quality Control Costs** The costs of ensuring that a firm's products are manufactured up to the desired quality, e.g., costs of inspection, testing, and correction of defective items or components. (see Failure Costs)
- **Direct Cost** Represents direct labor and direct material costs.
- **Discretionary** Costs Costs that can be determined by the management of a firm and that are not related to manufacturing, e.g., advertising costs.
- **Failure Costs** The cost consequences of producing defective or substandard products. They include rectification costs and cost of material, as well as the possibility of losing customers.
- **Fixed Costs** Costs that remain the same regardless of the volume of production, e.g., rents, cost of finance, depreciation (in most cases), etc.
- **Implicit Costs** The possible return or profit that a firm has missed by

using owned assets, like a building, in running its business rather than in some other profitable manner. It is a form of opportunity cost. Hence, a firm in such a case should include in its costs an amount equivalent to the market rent rate of such a facility.
- **Marginal Costing** A method of costing whereby only variable costs of labor and material are allocated to units of production to arrive at the marginal cost of producing a unit. The bulk of fixed overhead cost is charged to the particular accounting period regardless of the volume of production or revenues.
- **Opportunity Cost** A concept that denotes the cost of an opportunity lost in using a resource in a certain way rather than in some other more profitable manner; the difference in benefits or returns gained from using the resource in alternative ways.
- **Overheads** Costs that are not directly attributed to a unit of production, e.g., depreciation, rent, utilities, administration costs, etc; also called indirect costs. There are different methods of allocating such costs to units of production in order to determine the total cost per unit produced. (see Apportionment)
- **Fixed Overheads** Indirect costs that remain the same regardless of the volume of productivity, i.e., depreciation, rent of offices and facilities, administration expenses (in most cases), etc. Their impact on profitability is directly connected with the volume of production. The more units of production a firm generates, the less the indirect cost per unit, and vice versa.
- **Variable Overheads** Indirect costs, the total of which changes in proportion to the volume of production, resulting in an even overhead cost per unit, like sales commissions and costs of certain types of maintenance arising from usage.
- **Rectification Cost** The cost of correcting a manufacturing defect in a product in order to raise its quality and performance to the required standard. (see Quality Control Costs and Failure Costs)
- **Standard Cost** A total estimated cost of a unit of production which accounts for all cost elements relevant to producing it. That includes direct costs attributed to the unit of production as well as its share of the overhead costs anticipated during the accounting period for a budgeted level of output.
- **Variable Cost** Costs that vary according to the volume of production,

e.g., direct material and direct labor costs.
- **Replacement Cost** The cost of replacing a fixed asset, at current prices, when it becomes fully depreciated or obsolete.
- **Apportionment** (see Apportionment under A)

Cut-off rate A yardstick for deciding whether or not a proposed project should be undertaken. It is the minimum profit margin the project should yield to cover at least the cost of its capital.

D

Decision Tree A tool used for decision-making purposes in cases of uncertainty. It illustrates, in a tree-like manner, the alternative plans or approaches to the problem and the likelihood, consequences, or outcome of each.

Deflation The opposite of inflation; denotes the drop in prices in a country.

Delegation of Authority An arrangement whereby some of the duties of an executive, manager, etc., are imparted down the hierarchy to a subordinate. It aims at facilitating and speeding up operations, reducing workload of managers, and increasing satisfaction of subordinates who shall consequently be better prepared to take up higher positions. However, the delegating manager shall continue to have overall authority and, in most cases, continue to be responsible for the actions of his or her subordinates.

Demand An economic term that denotes the quantity of goods and services that consumers in an economy or market shall buy during a period of time for a given price. (see Market)
- **Aggregate Demand** The total demand in a market or an economy for a commodity or service produced by a firm.
- **Elasticity of Demand** A term widely used to denote the relationship between demand for a product and changes in its price. Usually, a lower price leads to an increase in demand, and vice versa.
- **Supply and Demand** A term depicting the relationship between the amounts of a product's supply, the demand for it, and its price. If different suppliers supply a product in larger quantities, competition shall surge, leading to a fall in prices. By contrast, if a product is supplied in quantities below the aggregate demand, it shall become a rare and highly demanded product, leading to an increase in its price.

Depreciation The gradual fall in the original value of an asset during its working life due to use and/or obsolescence. There are different methods of calculating depreciation.

- **Straight Line Method** The cost value of the asset less its estimated salvage value is divided evenly by the estimated life of the asset (in years).
- **Written Down Value Method or Reducing Balance Method** A fixed percentage is charged every year to the diminished book value of the asset until the asset is reduced to its scrap value.
- **Sinking Fund Method** An annual depreciation amount is determined using Depreciation Sinking Fund Tables, debited to the Profit and Loss A/C and invested outside the firm until the accumulated investment reaches the value of the asset less its salvage value.
- **Annuity Method** It assumes that the amount invested in buying the assets should earn interest if invested elsewhere. So, the amount of depreciation is calculated using annuity tables at a given interest rate. Interest amount is debited to the asset account.
- **Insurance Policy Method** The asset is covered by an endowment insurance policy over its life, at the end of which the insurance company pays the assured sum.
- **Reevaluation Method** The asset is revaluated at the time of the Balance Sheet. The difference between the cost value and the revaluation is the measure of depreciation. Appreciation is not taken into account.
- **Use of Mileage Method** The estimated life of an asset, e.g., car or bus, is set in terms of predetermined mileage rather than time. Cost of miles is calculated by dividing the asset's cost by that mileage. Annual depreciation is calculated by multiplying the number of miles the asset has run by the cost per mile.
- **Machine Hour Method** Similar to the Use of Mileage Method, the use of the asset can be determined in terms of predetermined machine working hours.
- **Production Unit Method** Similar to the Machine Hour Method, the use of the asset can be determined in terms of the number of units of goods manufactured.
- **Depletion Unit Method** Used for mines, oil wells, etc. Total quantity of output and its total and unit costs are estimated. Depreciation is calculated according to units of goods produced.

- **Sum of the Year Digits** Similar to the Written Down Value Method, it produces a decreasing depreciation charge by applying diminishing percentages to the cost of asset less salvage value.

Debt An amount of money that an individual or entity owes to another that results from buying goods, services, etc. on credit, or from borrowing money for various purposes, including financing investments or generating more capital for the business.

- **Bad Debt** A loan or amount due for services provided or goods delivered that is unlikely to be paid by the borrower or customer due to insolvency or any other reason.
- **Debtors** It denotes in the accounts books the amounts of money that individuals, firms, etc. owe to the firm for services or goods they procured or money that they borrowed.

Disciplinary Procedures The regulations that should be followed by management of a firm in case an employee breaches the firm's regulations, behaves inadequately, or performs unsatisfactorily.

Discounted Cash flow A technique used to calculate the present value of anticipated future cash inflows from a proposed investment by discounting them at a given interest rate in order to decide whether the investment should be undertaken or not.

Distribution Channels The means by which products are physically moved and distributed, starting from production sites and ending at consumers.

Distribution Ratio The percentage of Net Profit (after tax) that a company distributes to its shareholders at the end of an accounting period. The amount distributed is called "dividend."

Dividend (see Distribution Ratio)

- **Interim Dividend** A smaller amount of dividend paid by a firm to its shareholders on a temporary basis until a final dividend is decided and paid.
- **Dividend Yield** The ratio of the dividend per share to the current market price of the share.

E

Earnings Per Share A profit indicator that is calculated by dividing the net profit (after tax) by the number of ordinary shares.

E-business Stands for electronic business, and refers to the business that utilizes computers in its various operations.

Economies of Scale The benefits a firm derives from producing large quantities of units of production, usually by using highly automated processes. Such benefits are manifested in reductions in the average cost per unit of production in terms of material, manufacturing, distribution, advertising, and selling costs.

Economies of Scope The benefits a firm derives from utilizing its resources to diversify its products or services to include new goods and services. Thus, the average unit cost of both the old and new products shall decrease, giving the firm a competitive advantage.

Efficiency A measure of the manner in which a firm utilizes its resources to generate products or services. For example, the amount of output that a firm generates from a given number of workers' hours or a given amount of material reflects the firm's labor and material usage efficiency.

Entrepreneur Someone who establishes and runs a new business enterprise.

Equity The sum of ordinary share capital plus any retained earnings and reserves.

Exclusive Dealing An agreement between a firm supplying a product and retailers or wholesalers, according to which the former assigns the latter as sole distributors and the latter agree not to sell the products of competitors. Other forms of such arrangement include the agreement between a number of firms to deal only with the products of each other. Such arrangements are often considered monopolistic practices and are therefore prohibited by law.

Exclusive Distribution An arrangement whereby a supplier assigns the rights of distributing their products in a given market, territory, region, etc. to one wholesaler or retailer.

F

Feasibility Study A study that aims at determining whether or not a proposed project should be undertaken. It involves studying the economic and technical elements of the project to estimate its outcomes and return on capital, as well as its social and environmental impacts, in some cases.

Forecasting (see Management)

Franchising A strategy that enables a firm to expand without raising additional capital. It takes the form of an agreement between the franchisor (a firm that owns the trademark) and franchisees (entrepreneurs) whereby the former gives the latter the right to supply its products according to predetermined standards. The franchisees provide the capital for the venture (usually branches) and pay royalties for the rights given to them, while the franchisor supports them with expertise, advertising, etc.

G

Globalization A term used in several contexts: political, economic, commercial, informational, etc. In management, it refers to a strategy adopted by multinational corporations that entails spreading their operations worldwide to reap the benefits of new and diversified markets.

Growth In a business context, it denotes the expansion of a firm, either externally or internally.

- **External Growth** An expansion of a business by taking over, merging, or entering into a joint venture with another firm.
- **Internal Growth** A expansion within a firm that capitalizes on existing resources, expertise, excess capacity, etc. to develop new goods or services in order to increase market share or to enter new markets with the existing products.

Goodwill The amount by which the market value of a firm's shares exceed the value of its net assets. It results from a firm's reputation, performance, established customers, etc.

Governance The measures that govern the manner in which an entity should be managed. It mainly sets out the functions and obligations of the board of directors and their accountability to shareholders.

H

Health and Safety A statutory requirement that obliges employers to set and enforce rules and regulations, which ensure a healthy and accident-free work environment.

Human Resource Management (HRM) A branch of management that is concerned with the management of people at work. It includes the recruitment and selection of workers, training, wages and salaries, and the various other benefits of employment. New approaches to HRM increasingly view human resources as a capital and as a key factor for achieving the goals of the organization. Such approaches focus on motivation, human relations, etc.

- **Manpower Planning** A system of ensuring an uninterrupted supply of the right caliber of staff. In large organizations, it entails a complex array of steps and arrangements, including manpower audits, forecasting future manpower requirements, etc, and it takes into consideration factors such as expansion plans, technology shift, training requirements, etc.
- **Recruitment and Selection** The process of employing new workers with the right attributes, skills, experience, and knowledge to fill vacant post. It involves searching for suitable applicants, screening them, and then selecting the most suitable ones.
- **Appraisal** The evaluation of the performance of staff. It aims at identifying strong and weak points of individual employees, taking measures to improve their job performance and satisfaction, and determining their potential for promotion, pay increase, etc.
- **Grievance Procedure** The procedure that the management of a business should abide by in case an employee submits a work-related complaint.
- **Training and Development** Training is the process of enhancing the abilities, competencies, and expertise of individuals in order to improve their performance, satisfaction, and subsequently, their productivity. Development programs aim at preparing promising employees for higher positions.
- **Coaching** A training scheme whereby an experienced staff member trains another, usually a new or transferred employee, on the job.
- **Mentor** A skilled employee designated to provide direction and support for a trainee, a transferred employee, etc. as part of the latter's training and development program.
- **Induction** An orientation program designed to familiarize a new

employee with her or his job and the organization in general.
- **Arbitration** An approach to resolving disputes between workers and an employer whereby an impartial party, called an arbitrator, mediates between the two conflicting parties to reach a mutually acceptable solution. (see Collective Bargaining)
- **Accountability** The commitment of employees to execute their duties and to be responsible for their actions and behavior. It varies according to the level of the post and the complexity of the duties involved.
- **Collective Bargaining** The process of negotiating pay rates, working conditions, perks, etc. between representatives of the workers (usually unions) and employers or their representatives.
- **Competence** The skills needed to carry out a task in an established manner. It is a measure used in competency-based training programs where the competencies required to carry out a job are identified in order to design programs that equip the employees with the skills and knowledge they need. It is also used in recruitment and selection to determine the skills that an applicant must possess to fill a job.
- **Motivation Factors** The drives that influence the behavior, performance, and productivity of staff and lead to either job satisfaction or dissatisfaction. There are different theories on motivation, each viewing it from a different Depth.
- **Hygiene Factors** Refers to the needs of people that, if not fulfilled, shall lead to dissatisfaction, but if fulfilled, may not lead to satisfaction. Examples are pay, security, and working conditions.
- **Job Analysis** (see Analysis)
- **Job Description** Part of the contract of employment, it is a description of the tasks that form a job, the responsibilities and reporting relationships of the job incumbent, and the minimum qualifications and experience required.
- **Job Satisfaction** The degree to which an employee is satisfied in a job. It is viewed as one of the forces that influence an employee's behavior, performance, and productivity. (see Motivation Factors)
- **Job Design** As a noun, it is the way jobs are formed. As a verb, it the process of forming jobs. It entails grouping tasks that are usually related in some practical manner into jobs that can be assigned to individual employees. The way jobs are designed has considerable impacts on the

job incumbent's satisfaction and productivity.
- **Job Enlargement** A way of job redesign whereby more tasks, usually of the same (horizontal) level of difficulty, are added to the job. It aims at diversifying duties, reducing monotony, and improving satisfaction, performance, and output.
- **Job Enrichment** Similar to job enlargement, it is a way of job redesign, but it differs in that the tasks added to the job encompass a greater degree of difficulty and add more scope and value to the job. It can also be used as a tool for gradual career advancement.
- **Job Evaluation** The process of evaluating the merits and comparative values of jobs in an organization. It aims at assigning grades or rankings and determining pay levels for each job in a fair and systematic manner.
- **Job Grading** The process of assigning appropriate grades to jobs according to a predetermined grading system in an organization.
- **Remuneration** Wages, salaries, etc. paid to the workforce as compensation for their labor.
- **Increment** An annual increase in an employee's pay s scale, usually determined according to such factors as experience, years of service in the firm, and performance.
- **Incentives** A payment scheme that encourages employees to increase their efforts whereby the firm rewards its employees with extra payment in a manner proportionate to their production.
- **Redundancy** The dismissal of an employee when the job is not required anymore due to reasons such as re-organization, closure of certain operations, or winding up the business as a whole.
- **Discrimination** Unequal treatment of people, e.g., employees, customers, etc. on the basis of race, sex, religion, national origin, disability, etc. It is prohibited by law in many countries.
- **Worker** An individual hired by a firm, organization, etc. to carry out a particular work.
    1 - **Blue Collar Workers** Refers to manual workers.
    2 - **White Collar Workers** Refers to office workers.
    3 - **Grey Collar Workers** A scarcely-used term that refers to workers whose job nature or duties is a combination of both manual and office works.

I

Indemnity The amount paid by the insurance company to the insured as a compensation for losses or damages.

Industry The cluster of commercial or manufacturing enterprises that are engaged in producing related goods or services, e.g., the IT industry, steel industry, etc.

Information Management A system that utilizes the capabilities of Information Technology in collecting, collating, and analyzing data in order to present it in a useful manner at the right time to assist management and other levels of staff in making informed decisions. It may encompass decision support systems designed to provide the additional advantage of manipulating data to see the likely consequences of different courses of action.

Inputs The resources that a firm uses in order to generate products or services. They include workforce, funds, material, equipment, etc.

Insolvency The inability of borrowers to pay what they owe. It usually takes place when, for example, the liabilities of borrowers exceed their assets, or when their expenditure surpasses their sales revenues. In certain cases, according to the provisions of the law, borrowers may declare their bankruptcy.

L

Letter of Credit Used in international trade, it is a document issued by the bank representing the purchaser of goods (importer) to the bank representing the seller of goods (exporter) assuring him/her that once the goods are shipped and supporting documents submitted, payment thereof is guaranteed and shall be made by the issuing bank.

Liability A debt owed by a firm or a person as a result of borrowing, procuring goods or services on credit.

- **Current Liabilities** The amounts owed by a business to creditors that must be paid in the short run.
- **Contingent Liability** A provision made for a likely liability, in case it takes place, though its likelihood cannot be precisely predicted.
- **Debentures** A type of long-term financing. They usually take the form of loans secured against the assets or particular assets of a firm, and they are characterized by their fixed interest and long-term nature.

Linear Programming A planning and decision-making technique used for optimizing the utilization of limited resources for maximizing profits or reducing costs. An example of this is the use of limited production capacity for manufacturing different products with different profit margins. The technique helps in identifying the most profitable combinations of products.

Liquidation The process of selling the assets of a company due to insolvency in order to pay creditors. It can take place at the request of shareholders or by order of the court upon the demand of creditors.

M

Management It has been defined in different ways by different thinkers. A clear and functional definition of management was given by Henry Fayol, the father of modern management: "Management is to forecast, plan and organize, to command, to coordinate and to control" (Cole 2004).

- **Management by Exception** An approach which entails that the management information system within a firm be designed in such a way that only deviation from plans are reported to management to take corrective action. In practice, it requires a certain degree of delegation of authority, and in some cases, the task of dealing with minor deviations is delegated to middle management. This enables top management to focus on important issues where strategic decisions are required.
- **Management by Objectives (MBO)** An approach whereby managers set targets for their departments, divisions, etc. in collaboration with their superiors. It aims at achieving greater efficiency and providing motivation and incentive to managers and staff. Factors that may hamper the achievement of objectives and key result areas are identified and analyzed, and action is taken to eliminate or reduce their impact. Results are reviewed regularly and corrective action taken where necessary.
- **Management by Walking Around** An approach whereby a manager tours the workplace, talks to employees, discusses work with them, and observes their behavior, performance, and relationships. It brings managers closer to employees and helps them identify problems and the reasons behind them. It boosts employees' morale and dilutes communication barriers.
- **Elements of Management** These have been grouped in different ways and categories. Below are the most common elements or functions:

1 - **Planning** The process of formulating action plans for the firm. It entails setting goals and designing appropriate organizational structures and mechanisms for the achievement of such goals.
2 - **Coordination** The process of assigning work, responsibilities, roles, and resources in an effective and balanced manner to ensure harmonious functioning within an organization.
3 - **Motivation** The process of ensuring the satisfaction of employees. It entails taking measures to satisfy the needs and personal goals of employees to provide them with the motives and drive that lead to efficient functioning and rational behavior.
4 - **Control** Monitoring the performance of the organization to ensure that the desired goals are achieved, and taking corrective actions in case of variations from plans.

Marketing Defined by the Chartered Institute of Marketing, England as follows: "Marketing is the management process responsible for identifying, anticipating and satisfying customer requirements profitably." Kumar, 1990 adds, "It coordinates the resources of production and distribution of goods and services, determines and directs the nature of the total efforts required to sell profitably the maximum production to the ultimate user."

- **Market** The American Marketing Association has defined it as follows: "The aggregate forces or conditions within which buyers and sellers make decisions that result in transfer of goods and services" (Kumar 1990).
- **Market Segmentation** The process of dividing a market into segments, i.e., sections or submarkets, according to certain criteria. This includes dividing customers into groups or submarkets according to their social class, age group, etc. or dividing markets geographically into areas, territories, regions, etc.
- **Market Structure** The way that the various aspects of a market are structured, e.g., the distribution systems in place, competition, disposition of the product supplies, and consumers' characteristics and preferences.
- **Marketing Concept** A customer-oriented business approach that stresses the fulfillment of consumers' needs. (see Consumer Orientation)
- **Marketing Mix** The four elements used by a firm to market its goods or services, also known as the 4 P's of Marketing. They are product, price, promotion, and place. (see Chapter 4)

- **Concentrated Marketing** A business plan whereby a firm utilizes its resources and expertise for the service of one market segment, be it a geographical area, social class, age group, etc.
- **Differential Marketing** A marketing strategy whereby a firm customizes a different marketing mix for each market segment based on its characteristics.
- **Four Ps of Marketing** (see Marketing Mix)
- **Competitive Markets** (see Competition, Demand)
- **Equilibrium Market Price** (see Pricing)
- **Integrated Marketing** (see Integration)
- **Customer Analysis** (see Analysis)
- **Advertising** (see Advertising under A)
- **Monopoly** A situation where a dominant firm controls the supply of a product and, consequently, controls its price.

Mergers (see Amalgamation)

Memorandum of Association A document required by the concerned government authorities stating essential information about the company, including its name, objectives, address, legal form, capital, number of shares, etc.

Mission Statement A statement that describes the purpose of an organization and its objectives.

O

Organization
1. As a noun, it is an organized entity established for a given aim, or to achieve certain objectives; it is comprised of a group of people who share the desire to achieve those objectives, e.g., social clubs, companies, schools, government organizations, etc.
2. As a process, it is the act of organizing something. In management context, it is the process of organizing the operations within an entity. It involves grouping tasks to create jobs and grouping jobs into processes, functions, sections, etc., with the ultimate objective of forming an organizational structure for the entity. It also entails formulating policies and procedure to govern the various aspects of operations.
- **Bureaucracy** An organization that is characterized by strict rules, fixed policies and procedures, and a clearly-defined organizational structure and division of authority.

- **Organization Analysis** (see Analysis)
- **Organizational Behavior** A body of knowledge concerned with the study of the behavior of people at work and the motives, factors, stimuli, etc. that trigger and influence their behavior.
- **Organization Culture** The customs and common way of thinking that spread in an organization and characterize it. It takes various manifestations, e.g., jargon, leadership styles, practices, and conventions. It is regarded as a factor that influences the performance and behavior of staff.
- **Organizational Development** The process of monitoring the functioning and suitability of the organizational structure, identifying the revisions required due to changing circumstances and making the necessary modifications to ensure organizational effectiveness.
- **Formal Organization** An organization that has clear objectives and a formal structure, where roles are clearly defined and responsibilities are formally assigned.
- **Informal Organization** An organization where roles and reporting relationships are not clearly defined. Instead, individual roles culminate from group dynamics, and leadership roles emerge voluntarily.
- **Flat Organization** An organization design that is horizontal in shape and is characterized by a short chain of command and a high span of control (see Span of Control). It may not function effectively without a higher degree of delegation of authority.
- **Tall Organization** As opposed to the flat type, it is an organization design that is vertical in shape and is characterized by a long chain of command, long communication channels, a lower span of control (see Span of Control), and a lower degree of delegation of authority than that in a flat organization.
- **Matrix Organization** An organization structure in which the reporting relationships of staff are multiple. It takes different shapes under different circumstances. For instance, specialized staff provides specialist services and report to more than one manager in more than one department with regard to such services. In addition, they report to the manager in charge of that specialist service. Though it contradicts with the principle of Unity of Command (see Unity of Command), it has practical advantages, and it is workable under certain circumstances.

- **Line and Staff Organization** In this type of organization, the functions that are related to the core business of the firm are identified and structured as organizational units separate from the support functions. The former are referred to as Line and the latter as Staff Functions.
- **Hierarchy** The vertical pattern of an organization, which consists of different levels of management, supervisory, and other positions. The higher the position in the hierarchy, the more authority it has.
- **Span of Control** The number of subordinates reporting to a manager.
- **Unity of Command** An organizational principle that stipulates that a worker should not report to more than one supervisor. However, Matrix Organization (see Matrix Organization) is an exception to this rule.
- **Centralization vs. Decentralization** A centralized organization is characterized by the concentration of decision making at the top management level. By contrast, a decentralized organization features more delegation of authority to middle management.

Obsolescence The state of a product or an asset being outdated due to change in technology, tastes, etc. or when the product or asset reaches the end of its working life. It is a major consideration in setting depreciation rates for assets and in the valuation of stocks.

Operational Research An approach to analyzing complex operational and production problems by using scientific, mathematical, and statistical methods.

Outputs The products that a firm generates as a result of utilizing inputs like labor, material, etc.

Outsourcing A concept that entails procuring services, components, etc. from outside suppliers instead of arranging or manufacturing them internally. Its main advantages are that it enables a firm to focus on its core business and that suppliers can provide better quality products at lower costs since they are specialized and can benefit from economy of scale. Its main disadvantage is that a firm shall be dependent on another for the supply of goods or services, which may put the firm's operations at risk.

P

Patent A legal right given to an individual or a firm to the ownership and exclusive use, production, or selling of a new invention, e.g., a new product, idea, major enhancements to a present method, a new method of production, etc. Patents remain firm and protected by law for a certain number of years that varies from one country to another.

Payback Method A method of evaluating projects involving capital investments. It is based on estimating the annual cash inflows from the project for a number of years or during its entire expected life. The total cost of the project is then divided by the estimated annual cash inflows to arrive at the number of years it takes the project to repay its total initial cost (also called Payback Period). If the expected annual cash inflows are uneven, they are added up from year one upward until the total inflow equals the amount of initial investment, which leads to the payback period.

Portfolio A multifaceted term used to denote a selection, collection of something, or a group of people or items having something in common. In a business context, it is widely used to denote a collection of investments (e.g., stocks, bonds, shares, etc.). Other uses of the term include portfolio of costs, portfolio of products, portfolio of customers, etc.

Pricing The process of setting prices for a firm's products. Various factors influence a product's price, including cost of production, demand, supply, competing products, etc., in addition to the firm's marketing strategies. For example, penetrating a new market may require setting low prices to establish the product and gain customers. Subsequently, the firm may increase prices gradually until they reach the targeted level.

- **Administered Pricing**
    1. Prices that are established by suppliers. In certain cases, this is considered a monopolistic practice and is prohibited by law.
    2. Prices set by the government, especially on strategic or essential commodities, to protect consumers. In this case, the government allows suppliers to gain a fixed profit margin.
- **Bundled Price** A price set for a variety of products that are packed together in one bundle. Firms usually resort to this tactic in an effort to increase the sales of the less-demanded goods of their product mix, though it entails reducing the prices of the highly-demanded products.

- **Equilibrium Market Price** The price of a product when its demand and supply are equal. According to the supply and demand theory, an increase in the supply of a product, particularly beyond the demand for it, shall result in a decrease in its price. By contrast, when the supply of a product falls, particularly below the demand for it, the price of the product shall increase as buyers shall be willing or compelled to pay more for the product. On the other hand, the price of the product is a major player in this equation. An increase in price shall lead to a decrease in demand, and vice versa. This can be illustrated graphically by drawing supply and demand curves. The point of intersection of the two curves depicts the equilibrium market price.
- **Price Discrimination** The selling of a product at varying prices in different markets depending on such factors as demand, consumers' characteristics, volume of sales, prices of comparable products, costs of logistics in different areas, etc. In some cases, prices set for certain markets could be break-even or below-the-cost prices. Yet, depending on its costing systems or market strategy, a firm may benefit from utilizing more of its production capacity, penetrating new markets, or maintaining existing ones with highly competitive prices, recovering more of its fixed costs and subsequently increasing its overall profits.

Products Goods produced by a manufacturing firm or services arranged (produced) and delivered by a firm engaged in providing services.
- **Production**
    1 - The process of manufacturing, making, fabricating, creating, or generating goods or services.
    2 - The amount of goods or services produced.
- **Product Mix** The array of goods or services produced or sold by a business entity. A business may diversify its products to provide consumers with a variety of selections in order to boost sales revenues.
- **Product Life Cycle** The phenomenal four stages of the marketability of a product:
1. Introduction of the product in the market, which is accompanied by advertising and marketing campaigns.
2. Growth, which features an increase in sales.
3. Maturity, where a firm's market share is established, competition starts to surge, and new competing products enter the market.

4. Decline, where sales decrease to levels that depend on various factors, such as prices and attributes of competing products that entered the market, the marketing strategies of the firm, and the degree of its dependence on a particular product for generating its products.

Profit The ultimate goal of establishing a business (except for non-profits). It is the excess of sales revenues over the total costs of producing the goods or services sold (see Bottom Line). A firm incurs a loss when its sales revenues fall below its total costs.

- **Gross Profit** Sales revenues less costs of goods sold (not including overheads).
- **Net Profit** Gross profit less overhead costs.
- **Profit Margin** The firm's net profit as a percentage of its sales revenues. It is the product of sales revenues less total costs.
- **Profit-and-Loss Account** A statement showing the sales and other revenues of a firm during a period (usually a fiscal year), the expenses incurred, and the difference between the two. An excess of revenues over expenses indicates a profit. If revenues fall short of expenses, it indicates a loss.
- **Retained Profit** The portion of after-tax profit that has not been paid out as dividends to shareholders. Instead, it is utilized by the firm to finance its operation, new expansions, ventures, etc.

Protectionism A policy adopted by the government to protect its national industries from foreign competition whereby it imposes high taxes, duties, and quotas on imported goods.

Q

Quality Control The procedures of ensuring that the products generated meet predetermined quality standards in terms of such attributes as materials used, weight, size, performance, etc., as well as conformance to statutory requirements in some cases. (See Quality Control Costs and Total Quality Management (TQM)

R

Retailing The final stage of the distribution channel (Manufacturing-Wholesale-Retail). It is concerned with selling a product to the ultimate buyers, and is carried out by retailers or retail outlets such as shops, chain stores, etc.

Return The profit or outcome of something, e.g., an amount invested, resource used, etc., shown as a percentage or ratio thereto.

- **Accounting Return** A ratio used to evaluate the feasibility of new projects. It is calculated by showing the estimated annual profits from a project as a percentage of the total amount invested in it. If the expected profit matches or exceeds a firm's target profit, the project shall be undertaken.
- **Rate of Return** The measure of a firm's profitability, expressed as a ratio or percentage of the profits generated to the value of its assets during an accounting period.
- **Return on Capital Employed** The profit of a firm during an accounting period as a percentage of the amount of capital it employed during the period.

Risk The likelihood of incurring a loss. It is a factor that needs to be accepted by every business undertaking. It arises from the uncertainties surrounding decision making and planning, especially those concerned with the future. The term is also used to denote a hazard, the possibility of injury or damage, or to refer to a person or an element that poses a danger.

S

Sampling A method of making judgments or forming opinions or ideas about a whole, in terms of characteristics, behavior, tastes, etc. by analyzing parts of it. Selection of samples can be at random from the whole population or from subgroups of the population that have certain characteristics in common. The method of selection adopted depends on several factors, such as the purpose of the sampling survey, the degree of accuracy desired, and the available resources.

Stakeholders The groups of people who have interests in or are concerned about the functioning and impacts of a firm. They include shareholders, customers, employees, and the community at large. Each group of stakeholders has a distinct interest in the firm. Their interests could be overlapping or, on the other hand, one aspect of the firm's operations or performance could be of interest to more than one group. For example, employees are part of the community as a whole, and so are many shareholders. Shareholders are interested in profits, and so are employees, since the firm's profitability ensures continuity of their jobs and possibly increased pay. Both shareholders and employees, as part of the larger community, are concerned about the environmental impacts of the business, and so on.

Stock Inventories consisting of raw material, work in progress, and finished goods. The term is also used to denote shares in a joint-stock company or some forms of financial securities.

- **Stock Appreciation** The rise in the value of a firm's inventory, due to such factors as increased demand, decreased supply (scarcity), inflation, etc.
- **Stock Control or Inventory Control** The process of maintaining stockholdings at optimum levels that are consistent with production schedules, sales forecasts, and orders from customers, in a way that avoids shortages in supply as well as excessive stocks. The former is ensured by setting a minimum stock level, while the latter is controlled by setting a maximum stock level. The balance between the two is checked by setting a reorder level. When stocks fall to that level, replenishment of goods or material should be ordered. This process optimizes inventory costs by reducing the capital held in stocks and avoiding the waste resulting from dead or obsolete stocks. It also ensures availability of the stock levels necessary for uninterrupted operations.
- **Capital Stock** (see "Capital Goods" under "Capital")
- **Economic Order Quantity** The optimum and least expensive quantity of material or goods that should be ordered to replenish stocks. Several factors determine the optimum quantity, including ordering, packing and delivery costs, warehousing costs, cost of waste and deterioration, amount of money held in stock, quantity discounts, etc. Calculation of the optimum quantity is done through a model that uses mathematical formulas to account for all the factors involved.
- **Stock Valuation or Inventory Valuation** The process of attributing a fair monetary value to the stocks held by a firm at a given point in time, usually the end of the fiscal year. There are two common valuation

methods in this respect:
1 - First-in, First-out (FIFO), according to which material used in sold products is valued at historical costs (assumes the older items are withdrawn first from stores), while the stockholding at the end of the period is valued at current costs (the recent items).
2 - Last-in, First-out (LIFO), is the opposite of the former method. According to it, material used for sold products is valued at current costs (the recent items), while stockholding is valued at historical costs (the older items). The way stocks are valued has a significant impact on the firm's accounting statements, particularly the profit-and-loss statement, since the material cost is an element that influences profit.

Strategic Planning The process of formulating plans and devising measures by which an organization achieves its objectives. An organization needs to determine its vision, set its objectives, and then formulate strategies to achieve those objectives.

Suggestion Schemes An approach adopted by some organizations whereby employees are encouraged to submit suggestions for improving the various aspects of work, e.g., methods of production, working conditions, policies, etc.

Synergy The benefits of the collective action of different elements pooled together where the total outcome or value of the pooled elements, or the unbroken whole, is better or larger than that of the elements put to work or valued separately. Synergy can culminate, for instance, from diversifying a firm's products, where its expertise and other resources are pooled to generate new products and increase sales. A firm's goodwill is another example. It is a realization of the firm's value as a whole, which exceeds the value of its individual assets.

System A set of components, rules, concepts, etc. that function jointly as one unit, e.g., a plan, method, procedure, machine, etc.

Systematic Performed according to given rules, procedures, methods, principles, etc.

T

Tariff A tax or duty imposed by a government on commodities, especially those imported; the price or cost of something.

Tender A means of procuring goods or services at the lowest possible prices. The buyer specifies the quantity, specifications, and other conditions of the service and invites suppliers of such goods or services to submit offers accordingly. The supplier who offers the best price and commits to the other conditions wins the tender.

Total Quality Management (TQM) A management approach that emphasizes a company-wide commitment, at all levels, to the highest quality standards during all phases of operation. It emphasizes the quality of products as well as attention to customers and their needs. As such, it embraces a customer-orientation philosophy that focuses on the needs of external as well as internal customers. The needs of external customers are accommodated by ensuring the quality of the product sold, services provided, convenient delivery methods, etc. On the other hand, internal customers are the different departments and sections that interact and complement each other in generating the products. This approach asserts that each department, section, etc. is a customer of the others and has to be served accordingly. This gives individuals across all departments the incentive to improve the quality of the internal services they provide to each other, which leads to reduction in costs, wastes, time, etc. and improvement in the quality of the final product, which leads to the ultimate goals of customer satisfaction and increased profits.

Trademark A sign, image, or phrase specially designed and used by a business to symbolize a product and make it easily identifiable and distinguishable. Once registered with the concerned authorities, it becomes protected by law.

Trend The tendency of something, people, or groups of people to take a certain course, follow a certain direction, or adopt certain attitudes, habits, tastes, etc., usually as a result of or in line with certain influencing factors. Future trends can sometimes be projected according to past behavior and patterns, e.g., sales, though their accuracy cannot be guaranteed.

Turnover A term used in different contexts, such as:
1. The sales volume of a firm during a period, usually a fiscal year (turnover).
2. The percentage of employees leaving a firm during a specific period

(workforce turnover).
3. A firm's sales volume as a multiple of its average stocks (stock turnover).

V

Value
1. As a noun, the price or cost of something, or the degree of significance or usefulness of something (e.g., it is of great value to me).
2. As a verb, to value something is to appraise it; set or estimate its price, cost, or worth; or to emphasize its importance or usefulness. The term is widely used in conjunction with other words to denote the value that has been added or benefits derived by a firm, or a process within it, as a result of utilizing resources. Examples are value added per dollar invested, value added per employee, etc.

W

Wholesaling The second stage of a product's distribution channel (Manufacturing-Wholesale-Retail). It is carried out by wholesalers who buy goods from manufacturers in large quantities and sell them to retailers.
Work Study A systematic examination of a specific job or operation that aims at developing the most efficient method and improving productivity. It incorporates two main techniques, i.e., method study and work measurement.
- **Method Study** The systematic examination of the present ways of doing a job in order to develop more efficient methods in terms of time, effort, material, etc., improve productivity, and reduce costs.
- **Work Measurement** The use of time-study techniques to determine the time required for completion of a task or job. It helps in formulating production plans and establishing costs and payment schemes.
- **Clerical Work Measurement** A measurement technique concerned with measuring and setting standards and benchmarks for clerical works. Also referred to as Organization and Method (O & M).

Workflow Analysis (see Analysis)

Y

Yield The income generated or return received on an investment in shares, bonds, etc.

- **Dividend Yield** (see Dividend)
- **Earnings Yield** The net after-tax profit per share as a percentage of the market price of share.

Appendixes

A1: McNally High Frequency Words
A2: Statistics about Word Usage in the Book
A3: Past Exam Questions
A4: Writing Template

Appendix 1

McNally High Frequency Words

These are grouped in order of frequency:
1. A, and, he, I, in, is, it, of, that, the, to, was
2. All, as, at, be, but, are, for, had, have, him, his, not, on, one, said, so, they, we, with, you
3. About, an, back, been, before, big, by, call, came, can, come, could, did, do, down, first, from, get, go, has, her, here, if, into, just, like, little, look, made, make, me, more, much, must, my, no, new, now, off, old, only, or, our, over, other, out, right, see, she, some, their, them, then, there, this, two, up, want, well, went, who, were, what, when, where, which, will, your
4. After, again, always, am, ask, another, any, away, bad, because, best, bird, black, blue, boy, bring, day, dog, don't, eat, every, fast, father, fell, find, five, fly, four, found, gave, girl, give, going, good, got, green, hand, head, help, home, house, how, jump, keep, know, last, left, let, live, long, man, many, may, men, mother, Mr., never, next, once, open, own, play, put, ran, read, red, room, round, run, sat, saw, say, school, should, would, yes, yet, bus, apple, baby, bag, ball, bed, car, cat, children, cow, cup, dinner, doll, door, egg, end, farm, fish, fun, hat, hill, horse, jam, letter, milk, money, morning, Mrs., name, night, nothing, picture, pig, place, rabbit, road, sea, shop, sister, street, sun, table, tea, today, top, toy, train, water, sit, soon, stop, take, tell, than, these, thing, think, three, time, too, tree, under, us, very, walk, white, why, wish, work, woman

Source: McLean, Bernadette and Rosie Wood. TARGET Reading Accuracy. Barrington Stoke Ltd. (Copyright Helen Arkell Dyslexia Center), 2004.

Appendix 2

Statistics about Word Usage in the Book

Chapter 2 gives a condensed account on the issue of vocabulary and the phenomenon of a certain limited number of English language words appearing repeatedly in most texts to the extent that they constitute a significant portion of those texts.

This appendix illustrates the relevance of that phenomenon to this book. It also shows how you can write appropriately if you have the right discipline-specific vocabulary in addition to other general English language words.

Excluding the list of the Practical Lexicon, the lists of key words and phrases, and the charts and tables, the statistics in this appendix are mainly based on the text proper prior to editing.

Total number of words in the text proper (before editing): 11,855 words.

Out of the 250 common words, 88 words have not been used, e.g. bird, dog, cat, fish, etc. The table below depicts, in percentages, the frequency at which each group of words has appeared in the text.

162 words appeared 5,602 times, making a percentage of %47.25 of the text.	%47.25
Other 88 substitute words[1] appeared 1,630 times, making %13.75 of the text.	%13.75
250 words made up a total of %61 of the text	%61
Out of the Practical Lexicon (307 Words), 46 words[2] and their derivatives have been used. They appeared 353 times, making up approximately %3 of the text.	%3
A total of 296 words made up a total of %64 of the text	%64
The remaining %36 of the text is made up of general and other vocabulary words that, individually, have appeared less frequently.	%36
Total	%100

To understand the implications of these statistics, the reader needs to keep in mind that this book is a writing tool and its discourse is multi-disciplinary in nature. The individual topics have been discussed in a simple manner, and in as much general vocabulary words as possible. Therefore, and as distinct from other management-related works, the text proper of this book is not management-vocabulary intensive. Had it been so, the number of the lingo words and the contribution they made toward the remaining 36 percent of the text would have been more. On the other hand, the number of general vocabulary words making that contribution would have been less. However, due to the multi-disciplinary nature of the book, the remaining 36 percent of the text includes vocabulary that is relevant to other disciplines, like communication studies and psychology.

---

1 -These words are:
Depend, Discipline, Inference, Punctuation, Depict, Elaborate, Foster, Important, Spelling, Detail, Embrace, Experience, Significant, Grammar, Reference, Both, Common, Illustrate, Nature, Substantial, Concern, Constitute, Consider, Generate, Mechanism, Problem, Utilize, View, According, Challenge, Check, Learn, Study, Vocabulary, Remain, Tool, Focus, Recommend, Pertinent, Ambit, Context, Expect, Knowledge, Often, Reason, Trigger, Relevant, Discuss, Role, Case, Cover, Relate, Address, Example, Define, Essential, Determine, Note, Outcome, Exam/Examination, Aspect, Further, Component, Include, Number, Text, Within, Plan, List, Recall, Concept, Appropriate, Write/Written, Involve, Student, Professional, Material, Idea, Issue, Answer, Need, Present, Key, Point, Topic, Use, Technique, Question

2 -These words are:
Accounting, Activity, Analysis, Customer, Organization, SWOT, Average, Behavior, Benchmark, Objectives, Re-engineering, Communication, Company, Competition, Consumer, Cost/Costing, Demand, Efficiency, Forecast, Growth, Health and Safety, Human Resources Management, Training, Incentive, Information, Management, Planning, Motivation, Control, Market, Marketing Mix, Four Ps of Marketing, Organization, Output, Price/Pricing, Products, Production, Quality, Risk, Strategy, System, Systematic, Value, Method Study, Work Measurement.

The bottom line is that only 296 words, including lingo words, made up 64 percent of the text proper of the book. This confirms the findings of the studies quoted in Chapter 2 and supports the idea behind the Practical Lexicon provided in this book.

There is no doubt that the more vocabulary you possess, the more writing ability you should have. However, the Practical Lexicon provided in this book and the high frequency words quoted earlier, in addition to as many other words as you could add to your vocabulary, should provide you with a tool to write appropriately on almost any management-related topic.

Appendix 3

Past Examination Questions

Introduction:

Examination questions are of various types. In the context of this technique, they can be grouped into two categories.

The first category is made up of questions involving wider topics that encompass different issues and concepts. In this case, the Management Model helps in visualizing the relationships between issues and concepts; the Ambit, Depths, and the Key Words help in generating more ideas and subheadings within the topic; while the Practical Lexicon provides the essential vocabulary. Question number eight on strategic decision making is an example of these.

The second category is made up of questions focusing on a specific or narrow topic or issue, where specific knowledge, definitions, or details are required. The Ambit and Depths are useful in such cases, as they help in recalling relevant knowledge about the subjects; the Practical Lexicon helps with the vocabulary whenever necessary. Examples of these are the questions on TQM, the decision making process, and culture.

Further, the approach to the questions in this appendix focuses on the use of the Ambit, the Depths, the Management Model and Key Words, and the Concept of Association. It is obvious that the time-management element of the Examination Technique is irrelevant here. You need to practice the technique under mock examination conditions to master its usage and achieve maximum benefits.

Question 1

Distinguish between the two terms quality assurance and quality control, within Total Quality Management (TQM).

The Institute of Administrative Management (I.A.M.)
Effective Management

Approach: You need to know the specific meanings of the terms Quality Management, Quality Assurance, and Quality Control. Keep the action verb "distinguish" in mind; then define the term Total Quality Management (TQM) and highlight its significance to an organization. Then define the terms Quality Assurance and Quality Control and explain their roles within TQM and the differences between them. You may conclude your answer with a closing paragraph to summarize key points, which are, in this case, the key differences.

To this end, let us explore the aspects of the Ambit and the Depths to examine their relevance and how useful they can be in this topic. The following list illustrates this exercise.

The Ambit

ASPECT	QUALITY ASSURANCE	QUALITY CONTROL
Definition/ Identification	(Write your definition or compose it at the end of the exercise.)	(Write your definition or compose it at the end of the exercise.)
Spatial Aspect	An organization-wide activity.	Mainly at the production line.
Timing Aspect	An ongoing activity involving design, revision, etc.	Upon producing an item, part thereof, or withdrawing material for use
People Involved	Staff of various depts. including Production, Marketing, R & D, etc.	Mainly the staff of the Production Dept.
Reasons/ Objectives	To maintain quality standards of products or services.	To ensure that quality standards are met

ASPECT	QUALITY ASSURANCE	QUALITY CONTROL
The Way it Happens	Through collective efforts of functional depts. in the design of products and setting quality standards.	Quality Control staff inspect products, components, material used, etc. to ensure that they meet the specifications, and staff removes defectives for further action.
Outcomes "O"	Quality products persuade consumers to buy them, maintain, or increase market share, and ensures continuity of the company's business.	Prevents defectives from reaching the buyers and maintains the image of the products and the company.
The Depths		
Scope	Organization-wide.	Production line/site.
Factors	Include the organization's capabilities in design engineering and market research to establish consumers' expectations and preferences.	Inspection methods, the components and material used, machine settings, staff training, etc.
Comparisons	(see Aspects & Depths)	(see Aspects & Depths)
Elements	Marketing, Production, Purchasing, and R & D Depts.	Products, components, and material.
Forms/Types	N/A	N/A
Characteristics	(already identified)	(already identified)
Assumptions	N/A	N/A
Alternatives	N/A	N/A
Constraints	Regional quality standards, for example.	N/A

As can be noted from this list, the Ambit has covered the vital issues related to the topic, and have distinguished between the two concepts and identified the differences: QA is an organization-wide activity that engages all departments, while QC is confined to the production line; QA is an ongoing activity, while QC is conducted upon producing a product. The Depths, on the other hand, have shed light on certain angles, i.e., the factors, elements, and constraints involved. You can elaborate on these points and write your answer accordingly. You may use the Key Words and the Practical

Lexicon if you need to. Further, sound definitions of the two terms can now be composed based on the information produced through this exercise.

Quality Assurance, for instance, can be defined as follows:

An ongoing, organization-wide activity that entails the participation of various functional departments, including marketing, production, and R & D, and that aims at setting, revising, and maintaining quality standards of products or services with the ultimate objective of persuading customers to buy the organization's products, maintain or increase market share, and ensure the continuity of the organization's business.

Quality Control, on the other hand, can be defined as follows:

An activity that entails inspection of products, components, and the material used to ensure that they meet predetermined specifications and quality standards. It aims at preventing defectives from reaching buyers, with the ultimate objective of maintaining the image of the product and the organization.

Question 2

Outline the key factors that may influence the process of decision making.

I.A.M

Effective Management

Approach: One of the approaches to this question is to begin your answer with an opening paragraph highlighting the importance of decision making in an organization and the types of decisions, i.e., strategic, operating, and administrative. In the second paragraph, describe the process and the steps involved (the decision-making model). Focusing on the action verb "outline," summarize in the following paragraphs the key factors that influence the process.

However, this is a straightforward question. If you know the factors, there is no need to use the Ambit. If you do not, the Ambit and the Depths, in conjunction with Association, can help you identify the factors.

The use of the Ambit and the Depths is illustrated in the following list:

Aspect	Description
Definition/ Identification	A process that constitutes a part of our daily lives. In organizations, it is a major activity of managers, executives, etc. to determine appropriate courses of action
Spatial Aspect	We make decisions at home, the workplace, shopping centers, etc.
Timing Aspect	We make decisions all the time, in various occasions, and for short-, medium-, and long-term purposes.
People Involved	- The decision makers, e.g., managers, executives, etc. - Those impacted by the decision, e.g., employees, customers, stakeholders, etc.
Reasons	To determine a suitable course of action
The Way it Happens	Defining the problem or issue, collecting relevant data, developing alternative solutions, assessing consequences, selecting the optimum solution, and measuring results
Outcomes "O"	A course of action that solves a problem or addresses an issue at hand and that may have short-, medium-, or long-term consequences
The Depths	
Scope	In this context, this refers to the scope of the process. The process involves a time factor, i.e., short-, medium-, or long-term; and the significance of the decision in general.
Factors	(can be identified at the end of the exercise)
Comparisons	Assessing the alternative solutions.
Elements	(see "The Way it Happens")
Forms/Types	Strategic, Operating, or Administrative; Programmable or Nonprogrammable.
Characteristics	(see Aspects and Depths)
Assumptions	The process may entail making assumptions in case of insufficient information.
Alternatives	Identifying alternative courses of action/solutions.
Constraints	Include the authority limits of the decision-makers, organization's policies and objectives, etc.

Assuming that you failed to recall some of the factors, you can associate the information produced through the Ambit and the Depths to find out what you know about the topic.

Aspects and Depths	Decision-Making Factors
Outcome O	The consequences of the decision and their significance.
People Involved	Emotions of decision-makers. The impact of the decision on others.
Timing Aspect	Whether short, medium, or long-term.
Constraints	The importance of the decision. The limits of authority of the decision maker. Policies and objectives of the organization. Available data.
Alternatives	The possible alternative solutions.

You may now eliminate the overlapping information and write your answer accordingly.

Question 3

If culture is interpreted as **"the way things are done around here,"** what questions could you ask to identify the current culture in an organization?

I.A.M.

Systems & Activities

Approach: Focus on the words "questions" and "identify" in the question. Then examine the expression "the way things are done around here," which implies that culture is a manifestation of the organization's behavior in general. So, you are required to ask the questions that shall help you in identifying the culture. These questions correspond to the factors that shape the culture. If you cannot recall some or all of them, then explore the Ambit and the Depths.

Aspects	Description
Definition/ Identification	(interpretation is given in the question)
Spatial Aspect	Internal and external forces.
Timing Aspect	N/A
People Involved	Management, staff, and stakeholders.
Reasons/Objectives	N/A

Aspects	Description
The Way it Happens	It is manifested by the company's jargon, rituals, policies and procedures, staff attitudes, management styles, organization structure, etc. These factors shape the culture, which, in turn, becomes a manifestation of them.
Outcomes "O"	It influences the behavior of staff and the performance of the organization as a whole.
The Depths	
Scope	The organization as a whole.
Factors	(can be identified at the end of the exercise)
Comparisons	N/A
Elements	(factors)
Forms/Types	Roles Culture, Power Culture, Task Culture, and Person-Oriented Culture
Characteristics	(see Aspects and Depths)
Assumptions	N/A
Alternatives	N/A
Constraints	It is difficult to change, as some of the factors that shape it are beyond the control of management, e.g., background of staff.

Now you can extract the relevant questions from the information generated. As you are aware, the Ambit corresponds to the 6 Ws & O. These are the basic questions that should lead you, through the process of association, to the questions required. This process is illustrated as follows:

Spatial Aspect (where): What are the internal and external factors involved?

Internal Factors:	
The people involved (Who)	Management: What are the management styles? Staff: What are their backgrounds, skills, attitudes, etc.?
The Way it Happens (How)	What language the organization uses and rituals it follows? What goals it wants to achieve? What organization structure and communication channels are in place? What policies and procedures are in force? What technology is in use?
External Factors:	
The people involved (Who)	What is the role and influence of stakeholders in the organization? What competition does it face?

Forms/Types: Based on the answers to these questions, one can identify the type of culture in an organization, whether it is a Roles Culture, Power, Task, or Person-Oriented one.

You have now generated a number of questions that are relevant to the identification of the type of culture in an organization. You may now write your answer accordingly.

Question 4

   a - Define benchmarking.
   b - Illustrate how benchmarking can be used to improve quality.

I.A.M
Systems & Activities

Approach: This is a two-part question. Each part needs to be tackled on its own.

   a - So far, you have seen that various definitions can be formed by using the Ambit and, sometimes, the Depths. Benchmarking can be defined using the same technique.

   b - The Management Model, on the other hand, can be useful in the second part of the question. However, the information produced in the first part shall be useful in the second one as well.

Aspect	Description
Definition/ Identification	(shall be formed at the end)
Spatial Aspect	Comparing the internal and external performance of an organization with that of another one.
Timing Aspect	N/A
People Involved	Mainly include the skills, training, etc. of staff.
Reasons/Objectives	To identify better production methods, marketing strategies, distribution methods, etc.
The Way it Happens	Requires identifying the processes that need improvement, studying the methods of carefully-selected firms, and adjusting their methods for implementation.
Outcomes "O"	Improved methods, quality, and competitiveness.

The Depths	
Scope	Depends on circumstances and need, but includes methods, procedures, quality standards, quality control, purchasing, marketing strategies, etc.
Factors	N/A
Comparisons	N/A
Elements	(scope)
Forms/Types	N/A
Characteristics	(see Aspects and Depths)
Assumptions	N/A
Alternatives	N/A
Constraints	The reluctance of competitors to disclose their methods.

The answers:

a - A practical definition of benchmarking can now be formed in a way similar to the following: *Benchmarking is a process that aims at identifying the best practices in an industry in order for a firm to keep abreast with the same and improve its competitiveness in general. It entails selecting the processes that need improvement; identifying the industry leaders; studying their production methods, quality of products, marketing strategies, purchasing and distribution methods, etc.; and subsequently adjusting their methods for implementation.*

b - Recall the Management Model. Visualize the relationship of benchmarking to cost effectiveness, methods, technology, efficiency (material, labor, etc.), and Total Quality Management. Also visualize the way benchmarking is linked to feedback, objectives, and plans, and subsequently to products, markets, and consumer orientation.

Remember that the focus of part (B) of this question is the term quality. Highlight its attributes, i.e., product design, quality standards in terms of performance, material and components used, etc., in addition to warranties. Then explain how benchmarking can be used for improvement.

Question 5

Advise on how marketing research can refine the marketing mix.

I.A.M

Managing Marketing

Approach: You may start your answer by defining "marketing research" and its role in an organization. Then name and highlight the elements of the marketing mix (the 4 Ps), i.e., product, price, promotion and place, and explain how marketing research can refine them. To this end, explore the Ambit and the Depths.

Aspect	Definition
Definition/ Identification	A process concerned with investigating the various aspects of a firm's marketing strategy, both present and planned
Spatial Aspect	The markets, regions, localities, or countries in which a firm operates or plans to operate
Timing Aspect	Seasonal factors affecting demand and sales, for example
Reasons	To reveal facts about markets (where) and products (what); to identify consumers (who) and their characteristics, tastes, preferences, expectations, and geographical locations (where); to establish their reasons for buying the product (why); the price they are willing to pay (how much); the preferred delivery methods (how and where); etc.
People Involved	The existing market segments, i.e., age groups, social class, etc., that demand the product or should be targeted
The Way it Happens	By conducting market surveys through appropriate methods
Consequences	Satisfied, retained customers and a profitable business
The Depths:	
Scope	Includes markets and their locations, market segments, consumers, products, competition, etc.
Factors	Product, price, promotion, and place
Comparisons	With competitors
Elements (see Factors)	
Forms/Types	Common types are interviews/field surveys and questionnaires (can be online)
Assumptions	N/A

Aspect	Definition
Alternatives	(see Forms/Types)
Constraints	Include limited financial and labor resources to conduct intensive researches. Sometimes, interpretation of data poses a difficulty

You have so far produced a good amount of information about what is involved in marketing research as a process in order to describe or define it. In an elaborate form, you may define it as a process concerned with studying the various aspects of a company's marketing strategy, either present or planned. It entails identifying present and future markets, existing and targeted market segments, and the seasonal factors that may affect demand. It involves identifying the characteristics, tastes, preferences, and expectations of consumers, the factors that prompt them to buy the product, the prices they are willing to pay, and the delivery/distribution methods they prefer. The process aims at establishing and retaining satisfied customers and ensuring continuity and profitability of the business.

Further, you need to explain the role of marketing research within the overall framework of the organization. For this purpose, recall the Management Model and visualize the position of marketing research in the diagram, the way it is linked to feedback, objectives, and plans. Then name and highlight the elements of the marketing mix (the 4 Ps). Explain how the data collected through the marketing research can help in refining each of these elements.

Finally, explain how proposed changes (or refinements) to the marketing mix may sometimes lead to major strategic changes, e.g., elimination of certain products, abandoning a market, entering a new market, changing logistical arrangements, etc., which may lead to major organizational changes or a strategic shift in the direction of the firm.

Question 6

Advise how information can be effectively managed to reduce the problems of information overload.

I.A.M
Business Administration

Approach:

1. Briefly explain what is meant by information management, and highlight its importance in an organization.
2. Briefly explain the meaning of information overload, its causes, manifestations, and the problems it creates.
3. Recommend measures for the effective management of information to reduce the problems of information overload.

Answers:

1. In the Practical Lexicon provided in this book, information management is defined as "A system that utilizes the capabilities of Information Technology in collecting, collating, and analyzing data in order to present it in a useful manner at the right time to assist management and other levels of staff in making informed decisions. It may encompass decision support systems designed to provide the additional advantage of manipulating data to see the likely consequences of different courses of action." The significance and major benefits of information management are encompassed in this definition. However, additional information to enhance your answer can be obtained upon exploring the Ambit and Depths, as can be seen below.
2. Information overload is manifested by dispatching too many messages or providing too much information in a way that disrupts work. Its main causes include organizational defects, inappropriate or unclear communication channels and lines of command, and improperly designed information management systems. The large volume of undesired information received by individuals hinders their ability to focus on useful information. It wastes their time and effort and often leads to confusion and frustration.
3. To recommend measures for effective information management, explore its Ambit and Depths.

Aspect	Description
Definition/ Identification	(already given)
Spatial Aspect	Information should be generated in, processed in, and forwarded to the right place
Timing Aspect	It should be generated and forwarded at the right time
People Involved	The right people need to receive the right information and be adequately trained and advised on how to use it for the benefit of the firm.
Reasons/Objectives	To facilitate decision making, corrective action, responding to changing circumstances and formulating plans
The Way it Happens	See definition. In addition, the informational needs at the departmental and individual levels need to be determined in order to tailor the reports and other forms of information to these specific needs
Outcomes "O"	Correct and optimum amount of information to the right people to enable them take the right action or make the right decision at the right time
The Depths	
Scope	Information management needs to be an organization-wide system
Factors	Include organization structure; lines of command; communication channels; and functions of the various departments, and the informational needs of different levels of staff. They also include roles and responsibilities of individual staff; their locations; the time factor; technology and its cost implications; policies and procedures in force; the required controls (see Constraints); and quantity and quality of information.
Comparisons	Information should include, wherever applicable, relevant comparisons, e.g., actual vs. plans, with respect to performance of designated units during specific periods of time.
Elements	(see Factors and Comparisons)
Forms/Types	Information management now refers specifically to a computerized system of managing information
Characteristics	(see Aspects)
Assumptions	N/A

Aspect	Description
Alternatives	Depending on the nature of information and other factors like the level of staff, urgency of the situation, etc., various media can be used to forward the necessary information to the designated staff, e.g., e-mail, hard copies, direct access to designated locations in the database by designated staff, etc.
Constraints	Include technology in use; costs; skills of staff; legislation; ans nature of information. Constraints also refer to the measures and controls that need to be imposed to safeguard information from misuse or unauthorized access. These include: Designated personnel to receive specific information related to their areas of responsibility, unless such information is deemed necessary for all to boost communication channels. Use of passwords. Classified and statutory-protected information, e.g., personal data, to be accessed only by designated personnel. Clear policies and procedures, e.g., retention schedules, rules on e-mail use, disciplinary procedures, etc.

Now you have produced sufficient information to proceed with point (3) of your answer, i.e., the recommendations. With regard to the provision of information, focus on spatial and timing aspects, the people involved, factors, alternatives, and comparisons; focus on "constraints" with regard to the necessary measures and controls to ensure safeguarding and appropriate use of information. Then shed some light on how these measures and controls can help reduce the problem of information overload.

Question 7

It is essential to know, in some detail, the purpose of a form before one proceeds to design it.
Indicate **four** important questions that need to be answered in order to define the form's purpose, and give reasons why they are important.

I.A.M
Business Administration

Note: I have selected this question to show how the Ambit and Depths can help significantly in recalling even remote knowledge by relating, through the process of association, the Aspects and Depths to what we know.

Approach: The question implies that certain questions need to be answered before a form is designed in order to define its purpose (the key word is the "purpose" of the form.) You are required to:

  a -Identify these questions.

  b -Give, in some detail, the reasons why they are important.

Remember that this question is asking for questions. Since the Ambit corresponds to the six basic questions, let us see how it can help, along with the Depths, in identifying or recalling these questions. You can generate questions similar to the following:

Aspect:	Description:
Definition / Identification Spatial Aspect	A form Where the form shall be used, in which department or unit? Under what settings shall it be filled, e.g., over a counter, or in the comfort of your home?
Timing Aspect	How long should it take an average person to fill it?
People Involved	Who are the expected users of the form? What are their perceived backgrounds? What do they have in common? Who are the custodians of the form in the organization?
Reasons/ Objectives	For what purpose shall the form be used (e.g., to apply for a loan or a job)?
The Way it Happens	Shall the form be made available as a hard copy, mounted online, or both?
Outcomes 0	Do we aspire, for instance, for a form that can be filled easily by the users or one that inevitably seeks very detailed information (e.g., immigration forms)?

Aspect:	Description:
Factors	What factors that should be considered in the form's design? (See Aspects and other elements)
Comparisons	How similar, or different, shall the form be from other forms used in the organization?
Elements	What are the required parts and contents of the form?
Forms/Types	Online or hard copy, for example
Characteristics	What are the desired, or required, characteristics of the form in terms of design, contents, appeal, and ease of use?
Assumptions	What assumptions need to be made (e.g. a certain educational level on the part of users)?
Alternatives	Shall the form›s users be given the option to fill it, for example, online or in a hard copy?
Constraints	Are there any restrictions applicable to the contents? Is there any legislation limiting your ability to ask for certain personal data, for instance?

Through this exercise, you have generated many questions relevant to the purpose of the form and its design considerations. Focus on four questions that are important for defining the purpose of the form. To this end, the questions generated under the following Aspects and Depths are some of the obviously relevant ones:

- The people involved
- The Reasons/Objectives
- The Outcome O
- Comparisons
- Elements

Now explain why these questions are important for defining the purpose of the form. For example, one cannot design a form before knowing who is going to use it, and for what purpose (e.g., applying for a loan). Further, comparing the form with the other ones used in the organization can highlight the rationale for adding another one, and so on.

Question 8

Analyze the role and purpose of strategic decision making.

I.A.M

Managing Processes

Note: In this type of question, the Management Model, the Ambit, and Depths shall be particularly useful.

Approach: This is a multifaceted question. You should not be deceived by its apparent direct nature. One comprehensive approach is to:

- a - Explain the meaning of the term "decision-making."
- b - Describe what is involved in the decision-making process (the decision model).
- c - Highlight the types of decisions.
- d - Give a more detailed description of strategic decision making, its mechanisms, role, and purpose.
- e - Cite the decision-making tools and how they can help in this process.

For points a, b, and c, in order to avoid repetition, refer to Question 2 in this appendix. For point d, let us visualize the Management Model to recall how strategic decisions are fitted in it. According to the Model, strategic decisions are concerned with setting the vision, objectives, policy, ethics, social responsibility, and long-term plans of the organization. These lead to decisions related to the organizational structure and change, strategic direction, growth, products, markets, etc. Benchmarking, marketing research, and SWOT analysis, for example, are some of the feedback mechanisms that enable management to make informed decisions.

The question asks you to "analyze," i.e. explore the different aspects of the subject (Table 5.4). To establish their role and purpose, let us explore the Ambit and Depths of strategic decision making.

Aspect	Description
Definition/ Identification	Strategic decisions
Spatial Aspect	Internal and external factors and impacts
Timing Aspect	Long-term plans and consequences
People Involved	Made by top management, upon feedback from other levels within the organization
Reasons/ Objectives	To determine the vision, goals, objectives, and direction of the organization.
The Way it Happens	Decisions are based on feedback on the internal and external performance of the organization. Benchmarking, marketing research, and SWOT analysis are some of these types of feedback that provide the necessary information.
Outcomes "O"	Corrective action or strategic shift, etc. to address problems or adapt to changing circumstances.
The Depths	
Scope	Concerned with the direction of the organization as a whole
Factors	These include markets, competition, weaknesses, strengths, opportunities and threats.
Comparisons	(see Benchmarking)
Elements	(see Factors)
Forms/Types	(see Strategic)
Characteristics	(see Aspects)
Assumptions	Due to their long-term consequences, such decisions are rarely based on assumptions. Rather, they are founded on solid data, extensive research, and forecasts generated by powerful tools such as Operational Research (O.R.), for example.
Alternatives	Analyzing the alternative courses of action is an integral part of any decision-making process.
Constraints	This is an important factor, especially in analyzing alternative courses of action. Soaring competition, for instance, may hamper growth plans; availability of financial resources influences decisions on expansions, and so on.

Now you have generated many points on the role and purpose of the process. Elaborate on these to produce the required analysis. Then briefly cite the tools that help in decision making, e.g., Operational Research (O.R.) and Decision Trees.

Appendix 4
Writing Template Using the Aspects and Depths

Appendix (4)
Writing Template *(please copy and enlarge)*
Using the Aspects and Depths

Aspects (Ambit):

Definition/Identification: ....
Spatial aspect: ....
Timing aspect: ....
People involved : ....
Reasons/causes: ....
The way it happens: ....
Outcomes/Consequences: ....

Depths:

Scope: ....
Factors: ....
Comparisons: ....
Elements: ....
Forms/Types: ....
Characteristics: ....
Assumptions: ....
Alternatives: ....
Constraints: ....

Key Words

Added Value	Benchmarking	Change Management / Leadership	Competition	Control
Cost	Cost-Benefit Analysis	Critical/Creative Thinking	Customer, focus on	Cycles
Efficiency	Legislation/ Rules	Macro vs. Micro Level	Market Share, Growth, Segments	Marketing Mix
Performance	Productivity	Quality/Qualitative	Quantity/Quantitative	Risks
Roles/ Responsibilities	Safety and Health	Short Term vs. Long Term	Sources	Speed
Stakeholders	SWOT Analysis	Tasks	Technology	Total Quality Management

Bibliography

Baguley, Phil. Effective Communication for Modern Business. McGraw-Hill, 1994.

Cole, G. A. Management Theory and Practice, 6th ed. London: Thomson, 2004.

Krone, Kathleen J., et al. Handbook of Organizational Communication: An Interdisciplinary Depth. SAGE Publications, 1987.

Kumar, Pradeep. Elements of Marketing Management. India: Nedar Nath Ram Nath & Co., 1990.

Lorayne, Harry and Jerry Lucas. The Memory Book. Ballantine Books, 1996.

McLean, Bernadette and Rosie Wood. TARGET Reading Accuracy. Barrington Stoke Ltd. (Copyright Helen Arkell Dyslexia Center), 2004.

Merriam-Webster's Collegiate Dictionary, 11th ed. Merriam-Webster Incorporated, 2003.

Murphy, Herta A. and Charles E. Peck. Effective Business Communication, Grolier Edition. McGraw-Hill, 1987.

Acknowledgments

The author is grateful to the Institute of Administrative Management(1)(UK) for permission to reproduce past examination questions, and to the Helen Arkell Centre for permission to reproduce the McNally High Frequency Words. He is also grateful to college professor and training expert, Dr. M. Al Mubarak for his insightful suggestions, and for the brilliant artist and graphic designer Mr. Mutasim A. Wahab who has produced the book in this design.

---

1 The Institute of Administrative Management, Coppice House, Halesfield 7, Telford, United Kingdom, TF7 4NA.
Tel. +44 (0) 1952 797 396 www.instam.org.

About the Author

His multi-continent, 34 years of management experience includes, among other capacities, as educational program manager, training specialist, and business development manager.

He holds a Bachelor and Master's degree in business administration (MBA) from San Juan University. Fellow of the Institute of Administrative Management (I.A.M.) in the U.K., Alnoor is professionally designated as "Incorporated Administrative Manager" since 1985 and holds both the I.A.M's final qualification as well as the Certified Diploma in Accounting and Finance of the Association of Chartered Certified Accountants (ACCA) in the U.K.

During his services in the corporate world, he chaired numerous committees and task forces, re-engineered processes, and trained and mentored staff through their career paths.

He is currently working on other books.

www.ingramcontent.com/pod-product-compliance
Lightning Source LLC
Chambersburg PA
CBHW070144230526
45471CB00002B/510